This book is dedicated to the memory of my mother.
Charlotte Lee Mitchell
September 9. 1946 – May 3. 2008

It is with love and humility that I also dedicate this book to my only son Matthew Steven Mitchell. My two grand-children, Autumn Nicole Mitchell ,Matthew Steven Mitchell(M.J.) I hope and pray this book will open their hearts and minds in a positive way, by causing positive change. So they will become all they were meant to be in life.

This book is written for every person who wants a better future for themselves and others. This gives me the opportunity to give back and help those who I've hurt and taken from, help those who don't know what they want out of life, don't know who to trust, how to handle their emotions and most of all. How to love themselves.

I definitely can't forget the wrestlers and coaches, I've been blessed to coach and coach with. Thank you guys for believing in me even when I didn't believe in myself. I can honestly say; I love you all. I learned a lot about myself and how to handle people and situations while being coach. I really don't miss coaching in the matches. I miss the talks and crazy things you guys would do or say. It is awesome seeing what you guys have become, which has gaving me way more joy than any big match you guys have won. I just wanna say thanks for the memories and I love you all.

I wanna give a special thanks to the manager(K.T.), who made it looked like I knew what I was doing, when sometimes I may have been confuse or lost track of the match. Thank You soooooooooooooooo much xoxoxoxoxoxo.

My overall hope is the person(s) reading this book. Have a attitude and mindset, that no-one or anything can stop you from reaching your **GOALS** and **DREAMS.** Please Watch & Listen   https://youtu.be/_PUF-I9UKRM

2 Corinthians 9:8
God is able to make all grace abound to you so that having all sufficiency in all things at all times, you may abound in every good work.

COPYRIGHT © 2018. ALL RIGHTS RESERVED.

No part of this publication may be reproduced, distributed, or transmitted in any form or by any means, including photocopying, recording, or other electronic or mechanical methods, or by any information storage and retrieval system without the prior written permission of the publisher, except in the case of very brief quotations embodied in critical reviews and certain other noncommercial uses permitted by copyright law.

DEAR WRESTLING,

Our journey began when I was just a child from a small town in Maryland. From the moment I first felt you, I knew we were right for each other. I was inspired to study you, and I learned countless lessons through the seasons we spent together. You taught me to value hard work, consistency, self-belief, teamwork, and perseverance. I would follow you anywhere.

I left home and followed you to Colorado Springs. It was there that I truly learned you would accept nothing less than everything I have. You tested me and asked me to conquer immense challenges. In return, you gave me the opportunity to compete on your greatest stages. You brought me face to face with the warriors that I grew up idolizing. You have forged relationships that will last a lifetime.

I have always chosen you. We have endured winter snow storms and blistering summer heat. You have made me physically, mentally, and spiritually stronger. Your standard is excellence, and I've seen its power, driving people of every culture. As I look within, you are the constant reminder that I am capable of more. You have been a continuous truth-teller. You taught me to never protect anything.

There is nothing I can do to completely return all that you have given me. I know that you deserve greatness. I know that you deserve more. Every choice I make is a reflection of you, and this decision is no different. Your stories deserve to be told by someone who knows you, understands you, believes in you, and comes from you. Because of this, RUDIS is the only place for us to continue our journey.

KYLE SNYDER
RUDIS

WRESTLING is Believing
WRESTLING is Total Commitment
WRESTLING is Blood, Sweat, and Drive
WRESTLING is What Ever it Takes
WRESTLING is One Goal (STATE)
WRESTLING is What You Give (101%)
WRESTLING is a Brotherhood
On and off the mat
WRESTLING is Everyone's legacy
WRESTLING is a Sign From Above
WRESTLING is finding a way…
to Dominate

WRESTLING IS EVERYTHING

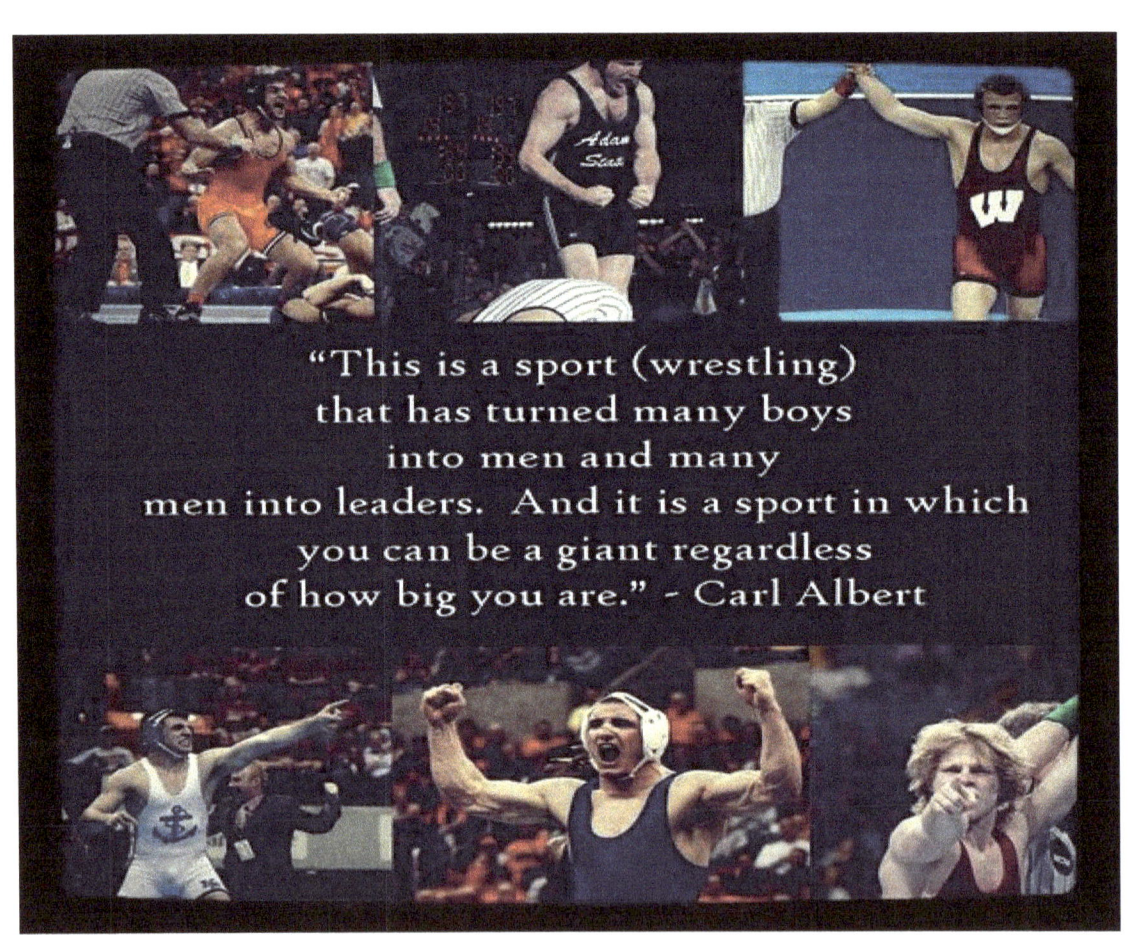

"This is a sport (wrestling) that has turned many boys into men and many men into leaders. And it is a sport in which you can be a giant regardless of how big you are." - Carl Albert

ALWAYS READY

Thoughts

are the

BIGGEST

killer

of

DREAMS...

Table of Contents

Introduction

1st Period

The Fundamentals of Wrestling to use in life..
3 Periods...
Flow like a river
A Wrestler's mindset
Basketball Player
The Decision.
First
Putting in Work...
Set yourself apart.
Can't...
Chances

2nd Period

Advice.
First Tournament
Can't make Chicken Salad out of Chicken Sh**
Take No-one for granted.
IF, I WISH TEAM.
Wall Chart
Pig-tail/Rat-tail
Starting Over.
Excuses.
Till I became one.

3rd Period

Instant Karma.
Sharing O.J.
High level.
WE ARE.
Vision.
Coaching.
The Program.
Million Dollar Question.
The Haunting.
Reflection of You.
When you want it MORE.
Why not YOU?
Knowing your OPPONENT'S
Team-mates/Friends.
Do What's Right.

Overtime .

Legacy.

Conclusion

In the END.

Bonus Chapter

Perseverance

Goal Setting

Vision Board

Wrestling is recognized as the world's oldest competitive sport. Cave drawings of wrestlers date as far back to 3000 B.C.

Introduction

My name is Timothy D Mitchell, I've been involved with amateur wrestling since 1981. As a wrestler, coach and official. There isn't much I haven't seen when it comes to amateur wrestling. I love this sport so much until I wanted to learn everything there is to know about this great sport. I'm also a person who has been through some things and situations. Some I caused, and some just happen to me when dealing with this thing called; LIFE. I'm just like most. I've had good and bad come my way in life. I've done many things that wasn't smart or right, for which I paid a price for. One smart thing I did, was joining the wrestling team in junior high school.

Not only is wrestling a great sport to participate in. This is one sport that will help you long after your wrestling career is over. Being a wrestler. I learned how to handle many situations that have come my way. I feel there's nothing I can't achieve or have anything to fear. This is a direct result from being a wrestler. This book is about me becoming a wrestler, how it relates to life and how wrestling has helped me on and off the mat(life). I hope to help any pre-teen or teenager, thinking about becoming a wrestler. I want to give some insight into what's ahead of them if they decided to join the greatest sport ever(Wrestling).

I will show, how a person doesn't have to be a wrestler to think like a wrestler. There is the saying that's used often and is so very true; Wrestling is just like life.

I will parallel the two, just to show how true this is. A wrestlers mind is unlike any mind on earth. A wrestlers mind fears nothing or no one. This is a very hard mind to break. Another saying is; wrestling is hard life is easy.

I hope to inspire not just wrestlers but everyone reading this book. I want you to believe in yourself, to be the best you can be in every part of your life. A wrestler has to be the best in every phase of wrestling. This book will teach you not to give up when things or going bad and also not be satisfied when things or going well. Just like in wrestling, things can change in an instant. As the same in life.

"Ready Wrestle"

The same lifestyle & Thinking in wrestling, can also be applied to your life. Everything in your LIFE should lead to living a happy, prosperous, fullfilling and productive LIFE... It's all pending on how you live your LIFE(LIFESTYLE).

1ˢᵗ Period

If you can dream it, you can do it.

Walt Disney

TODAY I WILL DO WHAT OTHERS WON'T. SO TOMORROW I CAN DO WHAT OTHERS CAN'T.

The Fundamentals of Wrestling to use in life.

Success in wrestling is a direct result of the wrestler's expertise in the fundamentals. After a wrestler has mastered the basic aspects of wrestling, then they're able to build on them to expand their wrestling repertoire.

Stance: Your body position and posture on the mat.

Good wrestlers, can tell if his opponent is going to be tough or not. By looking at their opponent's stance. Or the way he moves around on the mat. It's called reading your opponent.

Never appear to be broken. Walk with your head up chest out like nothing is wrong, even if your world is crumbling. Be just like the one commercial says; don't let them see you sweat. You will be surprised by the people watching you and want you to fail. When you're seen walking head-strong without fear, people tend to be intimidated by you.

Neutral Position: The starting position in which you stand face to face with your shoulders square to your opponent in the wrestling area.

In Life, you will face things, situations, and people head-on. Having the right mindset, knowledge of a situation and a determined attitude. You'll be able to face any situation or people you will face.

Level Change: The act of raising and lowering your hips to set up or execute an attack or to counter the moves of your opponent.

You always want to be lower than your opponent. This will give you the advantage in scoring. In life, you want to rise above your opponent, by gaining knowledge and wisdom to get the advantage over your opponent. Never stoop to someone else level if it causes harm or injury to anyone, especially you.

Penetration Step: The first offensive movement that puts you in a position to score. Wrestler's first step should be towards one another to set up a leg attack. When one wrestler is very good, and the other is not good at all. The one that's not good at all tends to back up or try to push the better wrestler away, for fear of being taken down to the mat. In which he does end up being taken down.

Whatever it is you're trying to do or achieve, let no one or nothing stop you from moving forward. You want to be the one that strikes fear in the people who are opposing you. Make them want no parts of you and back away from you. Make that penetration step and watch how far you go.

Take-Down: This is awarded to a wrestler, during which the opponent is taken down to the mat and gain control from the neutral position.

A lot of the things we face in life are not a person or thing. It's our **MIND**. Our subconscious mind to be exact. It's our biggest obstacle and very hard to beat. Whenever we choose to do something or say something, to better ourselves. Majority of the time our mind jumps in the way and give us doubt and fear. A lot of the way our mind works is through experiences from the past, which stay with us for the rest of our lives.

Once you get control of your mind and throw out all the doubt. You will have a much better life. In other words, take your mind down and gain control of it.

Referee's Position: The starting position in which one wrestler is in the top position and the other is on the bottom.

The wrestler in red is the defensive wrestler. You notice the head is up. Whenever a wrestler is in this position, he always wants his head up. This will better his chances of standing up to escape from the bottom. There is a true saying in wrestling; where the head goes the body goes. The wrestler in blue (on top) is the offensive wrestler. You see him forcing the head down. You see what's following. Look what happens when he gets his head back up and able to stand up and get away. Now he's ready to battle. Even though a wrestler can get back neutral or feet to battle. His opponent knows he must keep the pressure on the opponents head, and keep the head in a downward position to gain control. With the opponent putting pressure on the head. It makes him tired and wore him down. This makes it very hard for a wrestler to defend the attacks of his opponent.

You're going to come across people who want to get you down and hold you there. It will be people you don't know, casual acquaintance, ones who say they're your friend and there for you, even family members. These people will put doubt in your head, make you think less of yourself, whatever it is you're trying to do, to better yourself they will say it can't be done.

Their main goal is to keep your head down with low self-esteem, make you give up on whatever it is you want to achieve. Most of the time these people will be jealous of you because your strength is their weakness. Plus they can see your ambition and drive in what you're doing. They see things working-out for you becaue your hard work and a no quit attitude. Stay away from those types of people.

Remember:

When you're making a change in your life. Not everyone going to change with you. That's when you know you need to escape from them.

Escape: A move used from the bottom of the referee's position to escape or get away from your opponent. In life it's called; the wrong people.

Near Fall: If a wrestler holds his opponent back towards the mat.

In Life, it's called. Your back against the wall. When a wrestler gets caught on their back. They don't stop fighting off their back. I can't count how many times I saw wrestlers fight off their back, to end up winning the match. The key word here is; FIGHT. We all will have our back against a mat/wall. Just don't give up, keep fighting, adjust and do what it takes to get your back off the mat/wall. You will come out a winner.

Nutrition/Strength/Endurance: While the needs of a wrestler depend on a variety of factors, including age and gender, a good rule of thumb is to try to have the right diet, strong muscles and be in great condition.

You don't have to be a wrestler to do these things. These are good habits to have period. Since our number one opponent is our mind. We are going to have to know how to combat it.

Nutrition: Meditate, Pray, Read, Study and learn from successful people, Listen to motivational speakers, Focus on feeling good, Be Thankful, When possible give help and love without expecting anything in return, Learn to appreciate not expect.

Strength: Once you get the proper nutrition. You will have the strength to handle whatever the mind sends your way.

Endurance: You will have to make it a daily habit, of getting proper nutrition and strength training, to have the endurance to stay your course of what you want for your life.

Inspiration: External motivation and rewards can take you only so far; to be great in wrestling and life, you need to be truly inspired.

Positive Attitude: To be a successful in wrestling and in life, he/she must be in the right positive mindset, to win a match and win in life on any given day.

Strength in the Fundamentals: Great wrestlers understand the importance of the fundamental moves and work to improve them every day. We should want to improve something about ourselves every day. Look at it like this. If we improve 1% each day. In one year, we've improved 365%.

Style: Develop a style that fits their skills, strengths, and abilities. Each wrestler's style is different, so they develop theirs with confidence and then pay attention to the styles of their opponents so they can beat them. Find what you are best at. Always work to improve, to crush the people who may come against you.

Competition: Develop the desire for competing all the time, even at home and away. Maintain consistency in everything you do. Stay focused on the task at hand.

Mental Toughness: Understand that concentration, confidence, self-control, and goal-setting are all mental drills that wrestlers have to master to gain a mental edge. You will also need to have the same in life, in order to have the mental edge over your naysayers.

<u>10 Things Successful wrestlers don't DO.</u>
1. Make excuses
2. Have self-doubt.
3. Fear of Failure.
4. Procrastinate.
5. Try Pleasing People.
6. Fear of Success.
7. Negative Thinking.
8. Negative Self Talk.
9. Judge Others.
10. Have negative people in their circle

These are good habits to have in your daily life.

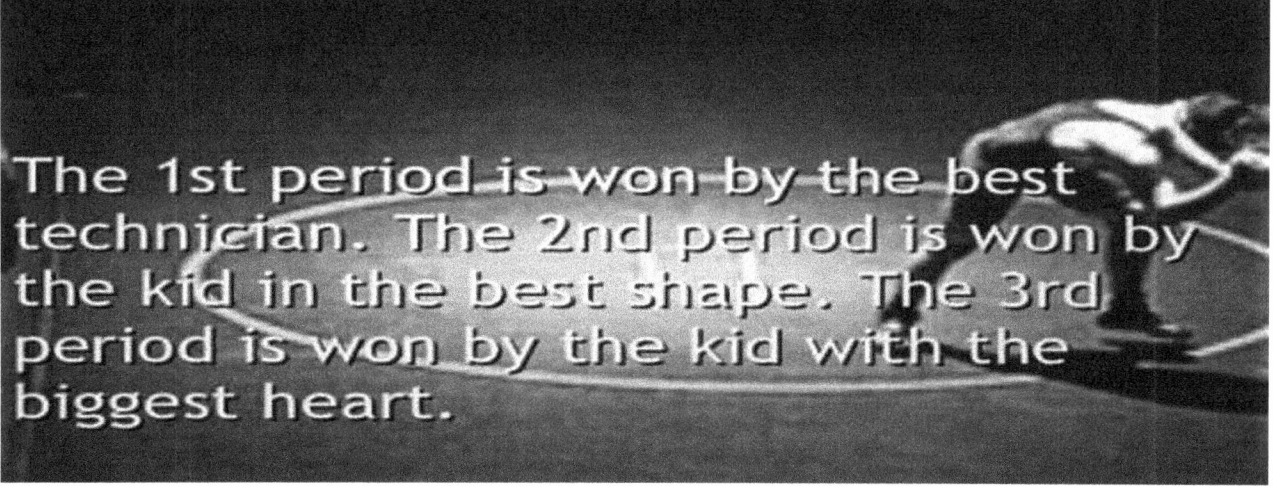

3 Periods...

Wrestling Facts
Serving Size: 1 Period
Servings Per Match: 3

Amount Per Wrestler	
	% Daily Value*
Total Commitment	365%
Discipline	122%
Desire	121%
Devotion	122%
Total Training	100%
Strength	20%
Speed	20%
Technique	35%
Strategy	10%
Endurance	15%
Overall Performance	100%
Mental Focus	85%
Physical Skill	15%
Endurance 100% ♦ Courage 100%	
Perseverance 100% ♦ Determination 100%	

Percent Daily Values are based on wrestlers willing to leave it all on the mat.

There are three periods in a wrestling match. There are also three periods in a wrestling career. The first period is elementary/Junior High. The second period is high school. The third period is the College. Some go on to wrestle on the world level. Which is a whole different level of competition, where very few succeed? So normally after College. A person's wrestling career is over.

Elementary/ Junior High, is where the wrestler learns the basics of wrestling. He is constantly learning and trying to figure it all out while making mistakes along the way. High School is where a wrestler is still learning. But is putting it all together from what he learned in elementary/ Junior High. This will form what type of wrestler he will be in high school. In college, the wrestler will still be learning, but he will still have pretty much the same wrestling style as he did in high school, but at a higher level to help him succeed on the college level.

According to studies. The average life expectancy for men is 76.4 years, while the average life expectancy for women is 81.2 years. When these studies are broke down into three periods. You will see what period you are in.

For men:

1st period is aged 1 to 25.4

2nd period is aged 25.5 to 50.9

3rd period is aged 51 to 76.4

For women:

1st period is aged 1 to 27.0

2nd period is aged 27.1 to 54.1

3rd period is aged 54.2 to 81.2

Everything after this is on a whole different level.

Life has; Young age, Middle age, Old age. What should be learned from a wrestler's career. Never stop learning, apply what you learn along the way to better yourself for every new situation you will face, never waste time on unnecessary things.

Because one day our career/Life will be over. When a wrestler takes his shoes off and leaves them in the middle of the mat. This signifies the end of a wrestling career. Very few wrestlers have this opportunity. Where will your shoes be left? In the middle of the mat or on the sideline? In other words, will you stand alone as champion or just be part of the crowd.

Law #24 in 66 LAWS OF ILLUMINATI...

Remember that the young shall one day be old. Be active. Prepare in the days of your youth for the days you are old.

SENIOR YEAR IS FOR THE TEARS, FACING THE FEARS, LOUDING THE CHEERS. YOU FIND OUT HOW CLOSE YOU ARE TO SOME, AND HOW FAR AWAY YOU ARE FROM OTHERS. YOU'LL HAVE YOUR LASTS AND GET READY FOR THE FIRSTS. THEN LOOK BACK ON IT AND REMEMBER IT FOREVER.

Flow like a river

My coach always told me. A wrestler should flow like a river. Meaning, you should constantly go from one move to another. No matter what your opponent comes at you with, it should never stop your flow. He said if you look at a river. No matter what's in front of it. The river will either go under, over or around it.

My 1st year wrestling. I drove my coaches crazy. I would be in a match, do a move then stop to look at them, to tell me what to do next. I knew what to do next, but I was unsure of myself. So I looked to the coaches to make sure what to do. A couple of times doing that, it cost me points and almost got me pinned. I did that my whole 1st year wrestling. My coaches and teammates kept telling me to stop doing that. I was too afraid to stop. I believed if I tried to win a match without asking my coaches. I would lose. So I created a dam named: **INSECURE!!!!!!!!!!!!!!**

That first year I went undefeated doing that. I carried that over into my first year wrestling in high school. That's when I heard the saying; **Flow Like A River**. I still looked to my coaches, to tell me what to do next in a match. That drove them crazy because they knew, I knew what to do next but still look to them.

There was this big tournament, where I had made it to the finals. I had my mind set on winning this tournament. I worked hard every day in practice to win this tournament because of how big of a tournament it is.

A little before I was to wrestle the final match. My coach came to me saying he had to make an important run. He would be back, but he wouldn't be able to coach me in the final match. I was instantly worried and begged him not to leave because I feared loosing the match if he's not there. He said to me. I would be just fine I know what to do, go do what you know, and you will come out a winner. I don't need him. He left just before the match. I said to myself what am I going to do? My crutch is gone.

All I can do is just go my hardest and see what happens. I ended up destroying my opponent. He didn't know what hit him. I realized after that match. I can do this on my own. I don't need a crutch. I went from being insecure to confident. By doing that I broke the Dam of **Insecurity**.

I had came to realize, as long as I put in the hard work and do what I have to do to be the best. I don't need someone else to lean on to help me win.

Hard work erases fear - *Michael Jordan*

Even when I lost a match. I knew it was because my opponent was better than I or I made mistakes. It wasn't because my coach didn't tell me what to do. When I referee the elementary and Junior High wrestlers. It's like deja vu, seeing them doing same as me. I say to myself; WOW!!!! I remember those days; they're going to learn as I did.

In the match of life. You will need people to help you learn and achieve the many things you want out in life. You will have to do your research study and read materials that will help you achieve what you want.

Once you have done everything, you can do learn and better yourself to achieve what you want in life. Don't let not having someone else besides you, telling you what you need to do or the dam of FEAR and INSECURITIES hold you back. You will hit a dam when you're trying to achieve anything. That's just a part of life. Remember this:

Dams are a barrier constructed to hold back water, typically found in rivers, and raise its level. The resulting reservoir is used in the generation of electricity, as a water supply or for other purposes.

A dam can is very useful. When you come across a dam or roadblock. Use that as an opportunity to learn even more and be better prepared. You will be surprised what you can do and realize you don't need something or someone lean on. It comes down to the outcome you want. Do what you have to do, to achieve what you want. You will be surprised at how unstoppable you are.

A RIVER CUTS THROUGH A ROCK NOT BECAUSE OF ITS POWER BUT ITS PERSISTENCE

The river you see at the beginning of this section is the beginning of Niagara Falls. When Niagara Falls is flowing at its full capacity. Nothing can stop it. You too can be like Niagara Falls.

"UNSTOPPABLE"

Don't worry about what you have to lose and start focusing on what you have to gain. Sometimes you have to let go of that safety net and see what happens. Then make adjustments, to get the results you want.

You have to overcome <u>YOU</u> before you can overcome them. Get out of your own way………

ONLY DEAD FISH GO WITH THE FLOW.

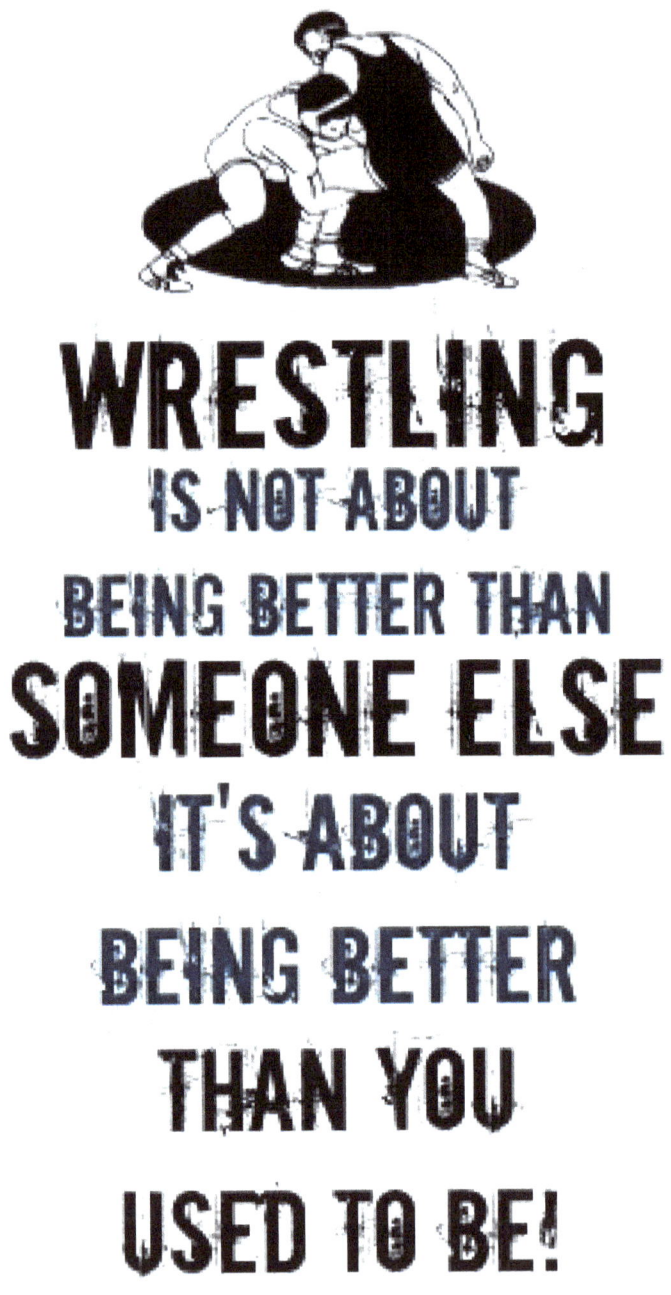

Strive to better yourself everyday...

A Wrestler's mindset.

Mindset: A fixed mental attitude or disposition that predetermines a person's responses to and interpretations of situations.

Nothing can stop the man with the right mental attitude from achieving his goal; nothing on earth can help the man with the wrong mental attitude..- Thomas Jefferson

A "wrestlers" mindset is unlike any other. He is programmed to destroy and put constant pressure on his or her opponent, both mentally and physically. It's them against the world he/she must win at all costs failure is not an option. I was told if a person lines up across from you with two broke arms and two broke legs, you break his neck. This sounds unfair, barbaric and evil, but all wrestlers are taught to destroy. Wrestling is not a friendly or prissy sport. It's the type of sport where you have to give it your all at all times.

In practice, in a match and even at home. You can always improve. If you're not working hard to improve, somebody out there is working hard, and you will have to face that person. The rewards for being a wrestler are astronomical. Knowing you worked hard to achieve success because you put in the work to make everything possible to be very successful. Even then success is not enough; there is always something to improve. A true champion will never settle.

I've said wrestling is just like life. You only get out of it what you put into it. If you let it, life will chew you up and spit you out. Never settle for less than life has to offer. Work hard to be the best you can be or be destroyed. I was told an old saying; life is not fair, so make it happen for yourself.

Just Know This:

Life is unfair, barbaric and evil. Depending on how bad you want something out of life. Will you be willing to put in the work to get it? If you're not, you're settling for everything less.

Wrestler's always want more and then some. You have to know there is much more you can achieve if you just have the drive to keep working hard to achieve it. Forget what you see on T.V. and infomercials when they make it seem like you don't have to work hard to achieve success. That's all a lie and for lazy people. Anything worth having takes work. You don't have to be a wrestler to think like a wrestler. Life is just like a wrestling match. But the match of life is tougher than any wrestling match.

The mind is everything. What you think you become.-Buddha

I DO NOT FIX MY PROBLEMS. I FIX MY THINKING. THEN PROBLEMS FIX THEMSELVES.

www.wrestlingmindset.com

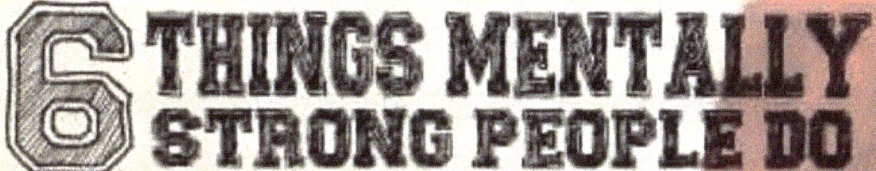

6 THINGS MENTALLY STRONG PEOPLE DO

1. They move on. They don't waste time feeling sorry for themselves.

2. They embrace change. They welcome challenges.

3. They stay happy. They don't waste energy on things they can't control.

4. They are kind, fair and unafraid to speak up.

5. They are willing to take calculated risks.

6. They celebrate other people's success. They don't resent that success.

Basketball Player

Before wrestling. I was a basketball player, so I thought. My junior high school had basketball tryouts, I made sure to attend. To make the team, you had to get past 3 cuts. I made it past the first two cuts, but not the third cut. When I saw who made the team, I was very upset. There were those who made the team that I was better than. I couldn't understand why they made the team and not myself.

I talked to the coach, to find out why I didn't make the team, and others did. He said the main reason why I didn't make the team, was because he didn't want my kind on the team. I asked him what he meant by that?

He said because I'm always fighting, getting suspended from school and causing trouble. That really crushed me. This turned out to be the best thing that could ever happen to me. After that crushing blow, a kid asked me to go out for the wrestling team, and my life had changed for the better.

I learned everything that may appear to be a failure is not a failure or a loss. Sometimes it's the best thing to ever happen to you. You may get fired from a job where you are the better worker, a marriage or relationship may end, or a so-called friend may have stabbed you in the back.

What it all boils down to is how you handle the situation. You can choose to stay down and have a pity party, or you can get back up, brush your shoulders off and move on. The odds are that when you look back, you can see that negative actually turned into a positive and was the best thing to ever happen to you. I remember losing in the State Finals of wrestling. I gave everything, I had to get to that point. I felt I deserved to be a State Champion. Even though that didn't happen. I gain much more.

Lost

1. Lost State Finals match

Gain

1.Never give up attitude. 2.Discipline. 3.Pride in myself. 4.College Scholarship. 5.Great friends. 6.How to handle defeat. 7.How to handle a bad situation. 8.How to handle stress. 9.How to diet. 10. Maintain a healthy body. 11.How to encourage others. 12. Who to listen to. 13.How to stay focus. 14.Self Defense. 15.How to be a visionary. 16.Mental Toughness. 17. There's a lot more to Hard Work. 18.A strong WHY I'm doing this. 19. Be creative. 20. Be ruthless. 21.Know who I am. 22. Politeness is a sign of toughness. 23.Set goals. 24. Underestimate no one. 25. Never be intimidated. 26. Leverage your strengths. 27. Ignore your weaknesses. 28.There's no off season. 29. I can't do everything. 30. All growth requires pain. 31. Use pain as motivation. 32. Complaining makes you stupid and weak. 33. Don't look pass anyone.

John Smith, Is regarded as the greatest wrestler ever. He even lost a match at the 92 Olympic Games. But was able to wrestle his way back to win the gold medal....

Most Notable Lost/Gain.......

1. Thomas Edison secretly conducted experiments in his office at Western Union that got him fired.

2. Steve Jobs was fired from Apple, the company he co-founded. His second act turned out to be bigger and better than the first.

3. Walt Disney's newspaper editor told the aspiring cartoonist he wasn't creative enough.

4. In the 1980s, Mark Cuban lost his job as a salesman at a computer store.

5. Michael Bloomberg used his severance check to start his own company. Now he's one of the richest people in the country.

6. Hartland Sanders was fired from dozens of jobs for his temper.

7. A Baltimore TV producer told Oprah Winfrey she was "unfit for television news."

8. Before being named NFL Coach of the Year, Bill Belichick was kicked to the curb by the Cleveland Browns.

9. Madonna lost her job at Dunkin' Donuts for squirting jelly filling all over customers.

10. Ford didn't want Lee Iaccoca, so he brought his ideas to Chrysler.

The Decision.

A real decision is measured by the fact that you've taken a new action. If there's no action, you haven't truly decided. - *Tony Robbins*

I've told you I was cut from the junior high basketball team. For being a troublemaker and fighter, who was always getting suspended from school. Then I had a classmate who asks me to join the wrestling team. It turned out he asked me to join the team, for his personal gain. He and some other wrestlers wanted me on the team, so they can beat on me and totally degrade me. The first day of practice they took turns beating on me, putting me in all kinds of holes and laughing in my face, telling me I'm not so tough now. This went on for a while. They made bets on how fast they will pin me or put me in certain holes. During school, while walking to classes they would tell me how they are going to hurt me today and beat on me to win a bet.

No matter how hard I tried, they still was able to run up the score and pin me. Then paid each other in my face. They knew they couldn't beat me in a fight. If I retaliated and beat them up, I would be suspended. So they had me. One day after a practice of being beat on and teased. I was faced with my first life-changing decision. I could quit and be teased, for being a quitter. Or stay on the team and keep being beat on and teased. It was a no-win situation. So the decision that I made which had changed my life forever. I decided to stay on the team.

I said to myself. I need to watch what they are doing, so I can learn how to do the same and use it against them. I asked my coach to help me and wrestle with me as much as he can. Within days of making that decision. The pens went away; bets went away, the matches got closer and closer, till they were barely beating me, to me winning by a small margin, then to me winning by a large margin. It got so bad, till they didn't want to wrestle me anymore. They became afraid of me. I took one of their spots in the starting lineup. Which he ended up never wrestling in the starting lineup because he couldn't beat me. I told you they would tease me during school. I let them have it.

Every chance I got. I was in their face telling them how they ain't nothing(sh**). I warned them how they better not come to practice if they don't want to get hurt. I had turned into a double threat for them. They already couldn't beat me in a fight; now they can't beat me in wrestling. I became the better Junior High wrestler and high school wrestler than them. They all ended up never wrestling in high school.

In life, you're going to be faced with many decisions, some bigger than others. The average person makes 2500 decision a day. You're going to have people saying you're no good. People are going to laugh in your face. You're going to be put down by people you thought was your friend, only to stab you in the back and hopes you fail.

A prime example of that. Is the friend of [Kevin Hart](). You will have co-workers constantly telling you that you are not doing a good job when you can clearly see you are. You can't quit the job because you have responsibilities. Family members are going to do and say mean things. There are going to be all kinds of things, that make you think, why is this happening to me. It just isn't fair. I learned a long time ago; life isn't fair. It all depends on how you choose to handle bad situations. Never focus on the problem. Focus on the salution.

Think of a strategy, where you can turn a bad situation into a good situation for yourself. Most of the time a situation that you may have thought was really bad, it really wasn't that bad at all once you worked it out. Most people will attack you because they see something in you, that they wish they could be or just plain don't understand. The main thing you have to do is not give up. Stay focused on what you want or trying to achieve. Don't let anyone stand in the way of your dreams and goals.

Obstacles come when you take your eye off your goal...

If you can't fly, then run.
If you can't run, then walk.
If you can't walk, then crawl.
Whatever you do, keep moving forward.

MLK

"You cannot become what you want by remaining what you are."
Get up every morning and tell yourself " I can do this."

First

Going into my first match ever in Jr. High, I was so nervous and afraid. After, I put my uniform on. My teammate's and coaches started laughing at me. I had put my uniform on wrong. I had put the tights over my singlet. My coach said this must be your first match? I was like YEAH!!! I didn't know it goes' singlet outside the tights.

If that wasn't embarrassing enough. The meet was held at the high school with 3 other schools there. With coaches and parents in a packed gym. It just so happen my team had the first dual meet of the evening. It was my team and the other team going against each other with everyone else watching our meet. That made me even more nervous.

When it was time for me to wrestle. Being so nervous and afraid. As I walked to the center of the mat. I trip and fell flat on my face. The whole gym erupted with laughter. I wanted to die right then and there. I got up, walk to the center of the mat with my head down. All I could think about was to get out this situation quickly.

When the ref blew his whistle, I went so hard at the may opponent until I pinned him in about 20 seconds. This was the only pin I had the whole season. Even though I had fallen flat on my face and everybody laughing at me. Word got around that I am a very tough wrestler. After that fall I went undefeated.

In my first high school varsity match. I was a wreck again. This time I didn't fall on my face. Since I was a middleweight wrestler, I got to watch the lighter weights wrestle. Our lighter weights were pinning the other school's wrestlers like nothing. While this is going on. My team-mate who was an upper weight said to me; we should pin everyone till we get to you. In which you'll get pinned because this is your first varsity match. But it's OK we'll still win the meet.

That crushed me. I believed he knew what he was talking about because he was an upperclassman and wrestled longer than myself. Again, I just went hard as I could. I pinned my opponent in like a minute. My team-mate who said I was going to get pinned, he got pinned. I said to him what happened, thought I was going to get pinned. He didn't like that at all. I also had a better overall season and career than him.

When setting out to do or be something. You're going to make mistakes because it will be your first time setting out on your journey. You're going to fall flat on your face, and people are going to laugh at you. Just know; It's not the fall that matters, it's how you recover from the fall.

People are going to tell you that you're going to fell because it's your first time or in a situation. Don't listen to that talk. Stay focus and go for what you know. You'll find the very people telling you that you're going to fell. Are the very ones you're going to pass-up, who have been doing it longer than you.

Denzell-Fail
Winners never quit, and quitters never win.

No matter how many people believe or don't believe in you. You must be the ultimate believer in yourself.

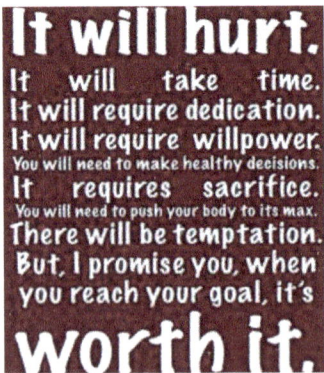

Putting in Work...

Great achievement is usually born of great sacrifice and is never the result of selfishness..-Napoleon Hill
Leave nothing for tomorrow that can be done today..-Abraham Lincoln

As a wrestler and coach. I came across wrestlers, who really didn't want to put in the hard work to be a great wrestler. They always tried to find shortcuts. One of the major shortcuts they tried to do, attend a big named wrestling camp over the summer. At these camps. Wrestlers will learn great moves from great wrestlers. Usually, these camps last a week. The wrestler would come back to summer wrestling practice, thinking they're going to whoop up everybody in the room. To their dismay, they still got beat and beat bad. They couldn't understand why they were still getting beat. I explain to them.

Your not going to be great in one week. I explain how it is great to go to camps. The best way to be a great wrestler is to wrestle, which is known in the wrestling world as; Mat Time. Then what you learn from the wrestling camp adds to your wrestling ability. In turn, making them an even better wrestler.

You see on the internet and TV some people are showing how a person can make lots of money without a lot of hard work or hardly any work. They flash cars, money, houses, clothes, eating at fancy restaurants, attending the best nightclubs and going on exotic vacations. All you have to do is sign up and pay for their program and then you can have all these great things. In most cases after signing up, a person finds that this program is not working and eventually dropped out of the program because it wasn't like it was advertised. In all these fast money making programs, there is always a disclaimer. Stating, if you sign up for this program, there is no guarantee you will make money. This is usually hiding somewhere in the commercial or in terms of the agreement.

Lots of wrestlers sign up for these wrestling camps based on a great named wrestler, who the camp is named after. There is a belief they are going to be great just like that wrestler only to be disappointed. In wrestling and in the match of life. There are no free rides. Anything worth having takes passion, hard work, knowledge, and wisdom. In wrestling is called; Mat Time. In life, it's called; Experience(Life).

The only place where <u>Success</u> comes before <u>Work</u> is in the dictionary.

TODAY I WILL DO WHAT OTHERS WON'T SO TOMORROW I CAN DO WHAT OTHERS CAN'T

We live in an Information society. Anything a person wants to know or get information about can be researched on a computer, tablet and even the cell phone. If there is anything you are thinking about attending or programs, you are considering to sign up and pay for do your research. In wrestling and in life you pay for what you don't know. For a wrestler, it may be a match. In life, it can be money, and everything you own and love. In other words; Knowledge is Power. Remember. Knowledge is what you learn. Wisdom is how you use what you learned.

> Through wrestling, through the hard work and the sweat, through the victories and the defeats, we learn a great deal about ourselves. Wrestling shows you your limits, your weaknesses, your strengths and, ultimately, you grow because of what it shows you.
>
> — *Jay Robinson*
>
> AZ QUOTES

"The same applies to everyday life."

Note:
When you only do what's expected. You will not have many special results.

Starting early and going long sends a message of commitment, purpose, and respect to others and yourself. Also assures better results over time.

Motivation: Is what gets you started. **Habit** is what keeps you going.- Jim Rohn

Here's a question for yourself. How much time do you have to invest in yourself?

If you say you're to busy with other things or just don't have the time. That's a lie you're telling yourself. Think!!! when you want something bad enough you will make the time and do whatever it takes to get it...

When you find your **PASSION** You never get tired, you passion fuels **YOU**.-Oprah Winfrey

Jay Z & *Dr. Dre*
What you do when nobody is watching is what separates a champion from everyone else.......

> every time **you** stay out late sleep in miss a workout don't give 100% you make it that much easier for me to **beat you**

Law #49 in 66 LAWS OF ILLUMINATI...

You should know your craft like the back of your hand...

Trust the work you put in.

Set yourself apart....

There are two kids both start wrestling at the age of 5. They're both on a club team. The one kid goes home after practice. Eat dinner, does his homework, play video games and go to bed. He gets up in the morning just before he has to go to school. Go's to wrestling practice after school and repeats the same thing over and over every day until wrestling season is over. Then he hangs out with friends, plays video games, watches TV and sleeps in on the weekends.

When school is out for summer vacation, he just hangs out with his friends, stays up all night, play video games and sleeps in. He doe's this year after year, till it's time to go to Jr high school. He wrestles for the Jr high team, repeating what he did in elementary. When he gets to high school. He decides to do a little extra to wrestle at the high school level. He may go an extra match in practice, run an extra lap and stay after practice if he has nothing else to do, like hang with friends or girlfriend. He wins a lot of his matches in high school but never can win the big or close matches. He just has above .500 record for his high school career. He lucks up and qualify for state tournament his senior year.

He gets an offer to wrestle in Jr college. Where he doesn't wrestle the full 2 years for the college. He ends up working a job that is just a paycheck to him, not rewarding or what he wants for his life.

The other kid stays after practice to have the coach work with him and show him moves that will help him improve. After wrestling club practice, he comes home to study videos of all the past great wrestlers to learn more. He does this until it's time to go to bed. He awakens an hour before he is to get ready for school. He works on the moves he can perform by himself(drilling). He does this till club season ends.

He finds another club team to wrestle for during the spring and summer. Along with wrestling for the clubs, he attends as many camps as he can. He wrestles basically all year round. It's a lifestyle to him. He doesn't wrestle in Jr. high because of his skill level. Junior high will decrease his skills. He practices with the high school instead.

He practices with all the top wrestlers around his weight class. He takes his lumps but is slowly getting better to the point where is beating the high school wrestlers, and he is not in high school yet. After he leaves high school practice, he still attends club practice and gets up early to drill on his own. When he gets to high school. He and some of his teammates get to school before classes start to drill. He attends practice. From there he attends club practice, wrestles as many matches as he can in the spring and summer along with club practices. He works on his skills 7 days a week.

He is pretty much untouchable. He wins all the big matches by a wide margin, which in the wrestling world is known as; DOMINATION. He knows how to win the close matches. He ends up being undefeated or at most have 1 or 2 losses for his high school career. He becomes a 4-time state champion.

He is wanted by all the big colleges. He gets a full ride scholarship to one of the big schools in wrestling. He uses the same work ethic as he had all the way up to college. With that same work ethic. He becomes a 4 time All American, and a national champion. He then goes on to wrestle at the world level. Where he is very successful. After his wrestling career is over, He is able to live the life he wants for himself, due to his work ethic and drive for success.

Both of these wrestlers started at the same time but did not finish the journey together. One wrestler chose not to put a lot of effort into bettering himself. Look at his end result.

As a coach. I had a wrestler come to me saying he was quitting wrestling because it was causing him to miss out on having fun. and it had too much work involved. I told him; you have a long life ahead you, put in the work now and you can have the fun you want later.

That didn't stop him from quitting. I saw him about 10 years after that. I can't begin to you how many times he said that was stupid and dumb of him to quit wrestling. He told me after he quit, all he did is just hang out with friends that he stop talking to after high school. He said. If he would have stuck it out for wrestling and worked hard, He said his life would be different now. He's not doing badly at all. But he realizes that his life could be much better if he made sacrifices early in life.

As you grow, you lose certain homies' —*Snoop Dogg*

When you see former wrestlers. Such as:

Dan Gable
John Smith
Tom Brands
Cael Sanderson

These are the wrestlers who made great sacrifices for wrestling and now living the life many people dream of.

You can also look at the life of:
Magic Johnson
Larry Bird
Michael Jordan
Kobe Bryant
These basketball players had insane work ethic, look at them now in retirement.

I keep saying, you don't have to be a wrestler or an athlete period, Whatever your passion is, strive to be the greatest. If anyone challenges you. You just destroy them. In other words, **DOMINATE** them.

Look at the Declaration of independence. You see John Hancock name stands out. You can standout also.

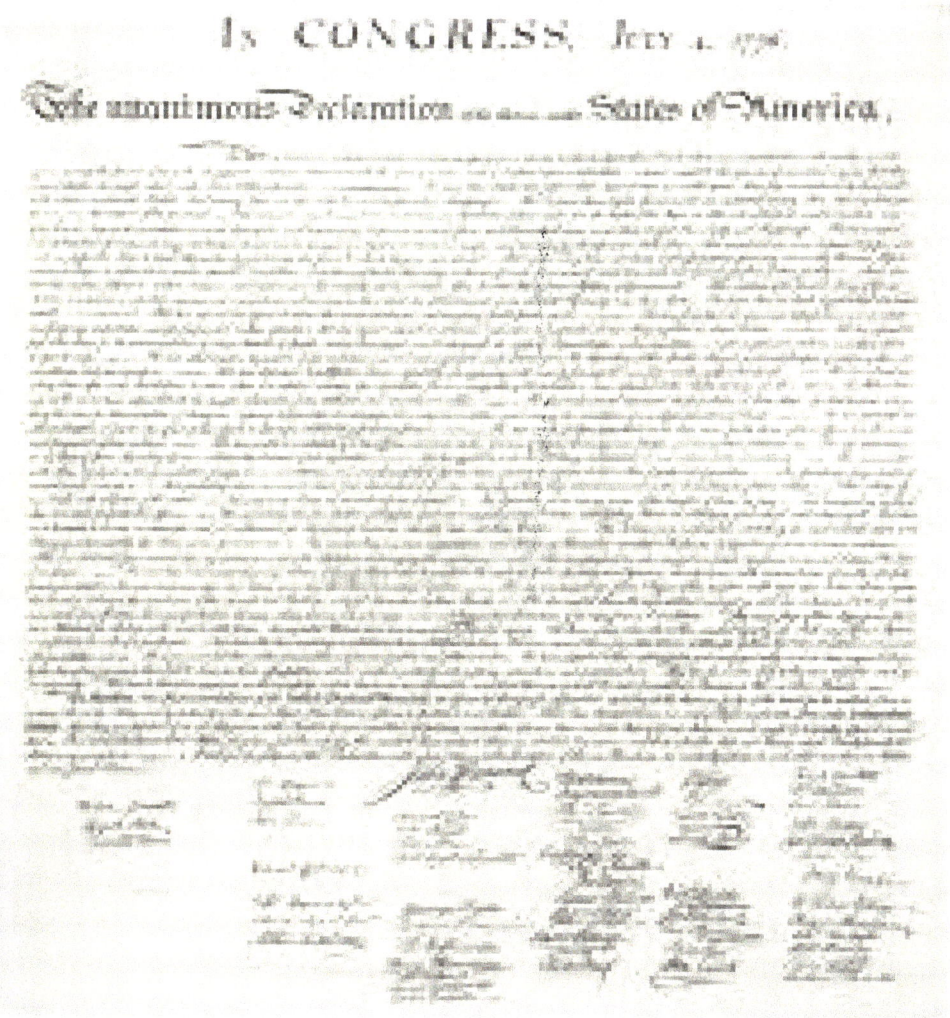

"I hated every minute of training, but I said, 'Don't quit. Suffer now and live the rest of your life as a champion.'"

Muhammad Ali

Note: If you think it's too late to go after what you're passionate about. Just know that Harland David Sanders, better known as Colonel Sanders(KFC). He franchised his first chicken concept at the age of 65.

Age doesn't matter: an open mind does. -Tim Ferriss

You can start late, look different, be uncertain and still succeed.

Law #51 in 66 LAWS OF ILLUMINATI...

Make excellence a habit. After the team finishes its grind, you must continue grinding...

The world ain't all sunshine and rainbows. It's a very mean and nasty place and I don't care how tough you are it will beat you to your knees and keep you there permanently if you let it. You, me, or nobody is gonna hit as hard as life. But it ain't about how hard ya hit. It's about how hard you can get it and keep moving forward. How much you can take and keep moving forward. That's how winning is done! Now if you know what you're worth then go out and get what you're worth. But ya gotta be willing to take the hits, and not pointing fingers saying you ain't where you wanna be because of him, or her, or anybody! Cowards do that and that ain't **YOU!** You're better than that!-**Rocky 4**

Can't...

Can't; is two words combined into one word. The two words are; can not. Meaning; not being able to do something.

To a wrestler. "**Can't**" is a sign of weakness.

A switch and sit out are two basic moves in wrestling. They both start from the same position. I was taught the sit out first. After a few tries, I knew how to do it without any problems. When it came to learning the switch. I was having major problems; I kept confusing the switch with the sit out. This went on a while. I hated when we would practice the switch because I wasn't getting it. One day in practice my coach asked me, What's the problem? how come you can't do this move?

I said. I just can't do this stupid move. He replied saying; this is a very good move, it will get you a long way and there is no such word as can't. I said to him, I will never use this move so that I won't need it. In my case, there is such a word as can't with my picture next to it in the dictionary. He just shook his head as he walked away.

I did keep trying the move, and I still couldn't get it. One day, it just clicked. I was able to do the move with no problem. It became one of my best moves. I added different variations to the move. I scored 99% of the time with the move. As a coach. I showed the many variations. One school name the move after me. I saw my high school coach; we talked about wrestling in my days. He said, I had one heck of a switch, that's what he mostly remembers of me. You can see. I changed the word can't, which is a short version of the two words; cannot. With the word "can." This is a pure example of not giving up. Keep trying. Eventually, it will happen for you.

I come across people who are dealing with certain problems or situations' that they feel they can't handle, can't solve or even do a certain thing to better their lives. Myself and others, who have been or had the same problems. Tell the person how to handle the situation, problems and even how to have a better life. Only to be told, they can't do that. 99% of the time, when asked how come they can't do it. Their reply was they just can't. After talking more on why they can't do a certain thing they would finally say, they just don't want to because there will be some discipline and work involved.

I saw wrestlers who wouldn't work hard in practice or push themselves to be better. But talk bad about the wrestler who is always working hard in practice, constantly pushing himself and winning matches. The same thing is done in life. It's just something that will never end. Always remember, your strength is another person's weakness.

People will attack you when you're doing bad. People will attack you when you're doing good and succeeding. So do what makes you happy and feel good. It's your life; no-one can live it for you. I learn as a wrestling referee. If I ref the perfect match. One coach is gonna love me; the other is gonna hate me. I just keep it moving. The one thing I never say is; can't. I changed it to; I know I "can." All you have to is BELIEVE.

Law of Attractions says:

What you think about, you bring about.

Matthew 17:20 says:

I tell you the truth, if you had faith even as small as a mustard seed, you could say to this mountain, 'Move from here to there,' and it would move. Nothing would be impossible."

Wrestlers are taught and believe. There is no such word as; can't because you "CAN."

We all get that voice of doubt whispering in our ear. Saying we can't do certain things that will make our life better. That's human nature.

Focus on the outcome. Instead of the current situation. Remember you can achieve anything you want. You just have to believe. 99.9% of the battle is just believing. Once you believe and change your focus, you will be amazed what you can achieve.

Don't be afraid to try.
Don't be afraid to fail
Do it.

Start now and make it happen, if you fail. SO WHAT!!!!!!

Eliminate the word CAN'T, and you'll be amazed what you CAN DO......

Don't cry to give-up cry to keep going.

Your words, your dreams, and your thoughts have the power to create conditions in your life.

Identify your problems, but give your power and energy to the solutions.-Tony Robbins

If you are insecure, guess what? The rest of the world is too. Do not overestimate the competition and underestimate yourself. You are better than you think.-Tim Ferriss

Chances

I coached this one wrestler, all four years of his years in high school. He was very good. Three years straight he had a winning record, won many tournaments, beat big name wrestlers. For some reason, he couldn't make it to state tournament. I felt so bad for him. I felt as a coach, I was letting him down and hurting his chances of making it to state. During the off-season, I was thinking if I should come back to coach or not, especially if I'm not helping him.

One day, I just sat down and thought about what can I do to get him to state. I figured out what we could do to make this happen, or I could just not come back as a coach. I took the chance to come back to coach him. If he didn't make to state this time. I at least wanted to say; I gave it my all. Deep down I knew I didn't want to go out as a quitter.

We changed some things. "Which" made it where we could just be focused on constantly getting better. Taking that chance, to come back paid off. He made it to state.

Then we had another problem. He needs to place in the state. A state qualifier is not enough for a wrestler like him. The wrestling State finals is a three-day tournament, where you have to win two matches before you lose two matches to be classified as an all-state wrestler. The first day of the tournament, you wrestle one match and then come back the next morning to wrestle, to get into the placing rounds on the third day.

What many wrestlers tend to do; is forget. After finally making it to the state tournament as a senior. Being so happy to qualifying for the state tournament, they forget to wrestle. In which they end up losing the first two matches. Which ends their high school wrestling career. He lost his first match. Nine times out of ten, if you lose your first match, you will lose the next one. It's a big uphill climb getting into the placing rounds. When I saw he was going to lose his first match. I started thinking again. What can I do, On top of that, I found out who he was up against the next morning. This wrestler was extremely good and had a very great chance of beating my wrestler. Plus my wrestler knew this kid and how good he is.

The only thing I could come up with, to help him win his next match. Was to take him straight out of the gym and not let him know who he had to wrestle or let him watch how the kid wrestles, to try and figure ways to beat this kid. No one around him could tell him who he had to wrestle next. I believed if he had found out who he had to wrestle next. All kinds of negativity would have gone through his head, which would most likely cost him the match, ending his high school wrestling career. I figured by the time he found out who he had to wrestle. It would be too late to think about all kinds of negative thoughts. Instead, he would say; the heck with it, if this is my last match. I'm going to give it my all. That's exactly what happened. He won that match and won his next three matches, which classified him as an All-State wrestler/State Placer. This same wrestler also loved dancing. He even missed a practice, to go dance at the school talent show. I was mad, which I let him know how mad I was. He told me it's something that he loves to do. I just said yeah okay. I was really thinking to myself he needs to give that mess up. After he graduated from high school. He spent the next two years, working by day and dancing in different night clubs.

One day I will never forget. He said to me he's moving to California. I asked why are you doing that? Then he replied, to become a professional dancer. I said; I thought you would have moved on from that by now. He said it's something; he loves to do, then he really got me, by using my own words against me.

He said that I always told him and the other wrestlers the team. If there's something you want in life; go for it. Let nothing or no-one hold you back, always push yourself to be the best at whatever you do; you have to just believe and stay focused. All I could say was okay, if it's something you believe in, go for it. On top of that, he was moving to California with really no money. I remember thinking to myself this kid has lost his mind. It turns out; I was the one who lost his mind.

He was handpicked by Beyoncé, to go on tour with her as one of her dancers. He has danced in many videos for Rihanna, Miley Cirrus, Michele Williams, Lady GaGa, Alexandra Burke, Leona Lewis, and many other artists. He danced at the Super Bowl, been on stage with Elton John, been on the show Glee, Nike tours. There is much more he has done, as a direct result from dancing. That dancing also lead to him having his own business, seeing the world and living a great life.

He took a chance and made it happen for himself.

Steve Harvey never wrestled. In these two books, you'll see he had many struggles to get where he is today. We see his destination and not his journey.

Steve Harvey- JUMP!!!

You can't fall if you don't climb. But there's no joy in living your whole life on the ground.

Whatever it is you want in life. Do whatever it takes to get what you want. If it's something you believe in, Don't listen to anyone who is not on one accord with you.

In wrestling, when you are trying to get to the top. You may get pinned a few times. But as long as you keep trying and learning from those pins. Instead of getting pinned, you'll be the one doing the pinning.

When you're trying to get to the top of the mountain in life. You will fall off a few times. Figure another way to reach the top. Instead of climbing one side of the mountain. How about climbing the other side and see what happens. No matter what, don't give up, stay focused. You will reach the top. The only one who can stop you is

The fact that you're not where you want to be should be enough motivation.

If your dream isn't bigger than YOU. There's a problem with your dream.- Deon(Prime-time)Sanders

CHANCES MAKE CHAMPIONS

Joshua 1:9

Have I not commanded you? Be strong and courageous. Do not be afraid; do not be discouraged, for the LORD your God will be with you wherever you go.

2nd Period

When there's no enemy within. The enemy outside can do you no harm..

African Proverb

FEAR- False. Evidence. Appearing. Real……

Fear nothing or no-one

Advice...

To kill a big dream, Tell it to a narrow-minded person.

Be yourself--not your idea of what you think somebody else's idea of yourself should be.-Henry David Thoreau

My first year in high school, I had a teammate who was a returning All-State wrestler. He was very tough and very vicious. In all my years of wrestling, he is the meanest one I've ever wrestled. He was so mean and vicious that a guy he was supposed to wrestle chose not to wrestle him, because how to mean he was. This guy beat the crap out of me every single day. When I would get up in the morning, I would do a countdown to butt whooping or a** kicking. I would say well 7 hours, I am going to get my a** kicked in practice, as the day went on I would say well I have 6 hours before a** kicking next 5 hours to a** kicking, all the way down to me getting my a** kicked in practice. My coaches felt so bad for me, years later one coach even said to me, I'm surprised you didn't quit.

One day while getting my a** kicked, the head coach chose to wrestle that teammate that always whooped on me. Mind you, my head coach at that time was an old man who wore canvas wrestling shoes, real tight clothes that look like a swimsuit; he was definitely from the old days of wrestling. So when he chose to wrestle him. I was thinking this old man is going to get hurt very badly. To my surprise, he beat the crap out of him, not only did he beat the crap out of him; he was toying with him like he was a little kid. I couldn't believe what I was seeing.

As I sat there and thought about what I was seeing, I said to myself; he is the coach he should be able to beat him because if he couldn't beat him, why would we listen to him. I found out. He's a Hall of Fame wrestler for the state of Pennsylvania and the University of Michigan.

From then on I listen to everything he said and taught me.

I learned from that day and still used to this day. If anybody is giving you advice or an opinion of what to do and how to do something. Look at that person and see if that person is somebody you want to be like or even should listen to.(*I for sure wanted to be like my coach*) Has that person succeeded at what you are trying to achieve, motivating or even paying your bills? In other words, what have you done or said for me to listen to you? If nothing, show them the **HAND** 🖐 and say **ANYWAY** or **WHATEVER**.

I've seen parents who do not understand the sport of wrestling but was always there motivating, helping, pushing their child to be the best they can be. Those same parents, made sacrifices, to help their child become very good wrestlers.

They would pay for their child to go to the best camps around the U.S. Pay for their child to wrestle on the best AAU teams. Pay for travel too many different states to wrestle in big tournaments. Whatever it was their child needed to help them be the best they could be they would do it.

Law #57 in 66 LAWS OF ILLUMINATI...

Surround yourself only with those who are walking the path of light. Successful people don't hang around broke people...

I've had Parents who would let their child wrestle but only to a certain point. When it came to doing extra to better their child, such as wrestling over the summer, wrestling for different AAU teams, going to camps. I was told their child does not need all this wrestling stuff. He needs to get into the books, to get a college education. This wrestling is not going to do that.

I explain to those parents that doing all these extra things will make them a better wrestler, it will also help in their academics. The way a wrestlers mind works is that he or she is not going to let anything or anyone beat them, including school work. Wrestlers will strive not only to dominate the person he or she is wrestling. Also, strive to dominate in the classroom. By being the smartest in the classroom. Studies show wrestlers are some of the smartest athletes. Many wrestlers go on to do very well in life when their wrestling career is over. There are many wrestlers, who are doctors, lawyers, own and run big businesses.

Jim Jordan is a U.S. Senator. One wrestler became President of the United States(Abraham Lincoln). I myself have coached kids who become doctors, lawyers, professors,NASA engineers, own and operate profitable businesses, graduate from West Point and Air Force Academy. I even have one who studies bugs for allergies in humans. After informing these parents about the other benefits of wrestling. They still didn't want their child to do all those things to help their child be better which could also pay for some if not all of their child's education. After their child graduated. The parents themselves came to me, saying why they didn't want to do all those things. They said. They didn't want the extra responsibility. I thought to myself saying, WOW!!!!! I had a very talented wrestler who lived in a low-income area; I talked to his mother about him wrestling in college to receive a free education. She told me her son doesn't need this wrestling sh**. He needs to go sell drugs and bring some money into this house. That was said to me by many parents in that particular area. It is what is known as a generational curse. Meaning how your parents lived. Chances are you will live the same way. It's all you know and ever seen growing up.

A person doesn't have to know exactly what you are doing or trying to achieve. They just know, it's something positive and your passion. They will push you to be the best you can be. Reminding you. You can do this because you have greatness in you. They will help you as much as they can and know-how.

I saw a Will Smith posted on social media. He posted a video saying always look at the people around you. Are these people fanning your flames? I say you want people who pour gas on your flames. Someone like Drew "Bundini" Brown. This man was Muhammad Ali's hype man. He didn't know a lot about boxing. He knew how to make Ali believe in himself by constantly reminding him how great he is, Greatest Of All Time(G.O.A.T.). He also came up with that quote: Float Like a Butterfly Sting Like a Bee. You don't need people, who is just there not helping you improve yourself. They're not trying to hold you back. They're not helping by saying they see no future in what you are trying to achieve. You definitely, don't want somebody around you. Who see no use in you trying to better yourself. Due to the way they are living and only know how to live a certain way.

Wrestlers always want the best around them as far as coaches, mentors and teammates. They know when obstacles come, there will always be somebody there to help motivate and remind them of their greatness, help better the situation and problem.

What you surround yourself with and actively engage in can affect your spirit. Be a partaker of good, positive, uplifting, Godly things, and motivate those around you to do the same. A big part of becoming an adult is unlearning a lot of the crap you were taught by people who didn't know what they were doing either.

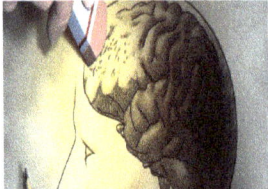

Know this:
Most people are fast to stop you before you get started but hesitate to get in the way if you're moving.-Tim Ferriss

Show me your crowd I'll show you, your future.

Keep no company around that you cannot build with or learn from.

DON'T LET NOBODY TAKE YOU BACK TO A LEVEL THAT YOU'VE ALREADY LEVELED UP FROM.

Watch/Listen: Steve Harvey-Flea

How you make others feel about themselves says a lot about you.

MAKE SURE EVERYBODY IN YOUR "BOAT" IS ROWING AND NOT DRILLING HOLES WHEN YOU'RE NOT LOOKING.

KNOW YOUR CIRCLE

🪔 A dead battery can't jump another dead battery..Get away from people who can't charge your spirit when you need a jump ! 🪔

First Tournament

My very first tournament in the High School was an eye-opener, to say the least. My team and I had walked into the school gym for the tournament. Most all the wrestlers from the other schools that were already in the gym. Seen us walk in started whispering to each other saying; I didn't know they were going to be here. They were so worried about us; they wanted to know what weight each one of our wrestlers was going. Some had said well we know who's going to win this tournament. Back then in those days, you weighed in, and your weight was written on your hand. I have never seen so many people staring at someone else hand like I did that day. I saw doubt, I saw fear and worry all in one day. Needless to say, we walked away with that tournament, then the following week the J.V. team won the same tournament. I remember hearing a kid say, wow there J.V. and varsity won this tournament. They're awesome.

From then on, I noticed something. All the wrestlers, I didn't know about, at meets and tournaments. Wore their wrestling medals on their jackets, which most of them was 3rd, 4th, 5th place medals. Never really seeing any championship medals. Or any major tournament medals. You could hear them before you could see them, do to all those medals rattling against each other. It reminded me of an old saying, I was told as a child. The loudest one in the room is the weakest one in the room.

All the tough wrestlers I knew about. Who was extremely good, winning all the major tournaments, placing in the states, being ranked in the state, beating rank guys and most feared. None of them had metals on their jackets; They were always quite, only talked if they just had to. (The 1st rule in laws of Power. If you want to control someone. Say nothing at all.) Still, people knew who they were, because of what they did on the mat and word got around. Back in those days, there was no internet, Facebook, twitter, Instagram or YouTube.

When these wrestler's walk into a locker room or gym. Other wrestlers were automatically afraid. It wasn't the metals on the jacket that made them afraid; it was what they did on the mat is what struck fear in other wrestlers. When I saw wrestlers with a lot of medals on their jacket. My teammates and I would go up to them and laugh in their face, and totally disrespect them. Calling them a joke and a sorry piece of nothing.

Know this; Confidence is silent. Insecurities are loud. When you're setting out to do something great or big. You don't have to broadcast it. When you are doing it better than others, word will get around. People you don't even know will know who you are, because of what you have achieved and how you are doing it better than everyone else. You will strike fear in people when you walk in a room. When you're doing it less than others, they will laugh at you and call you a joke and a piece of nothing. Be the best at whatever you do. All the great ones work harder than the rest.

They train harder, they learn more, they put themselves through more pain, more failures, more no's, more rejections if the norm is 12 you do 24 if the norm is 50 you do 100. Most all the great ones have talent, but that talent wouldn't be recognized as great if they didn't put in the work.

There are those with little talent, who have turned that little talent into greatness, because of a great effort. An effort will get you what you want in life. We all have a fighting spirit inside of us. When life has you on your back, you can't give up, Keep fighting off your back. Don't let people and things hold you back, from achieving what you want out of life. If you want more than most, you have to work harder than most, work smarter than most, learn more than most. Get off your back again and again. Make the sacrifices, create a great work ethic, don't stop keep pushing forward no matter what. Bottom line. Do what you have to do to be the BEST!!!!!!!!!!!!!

Can't make Chicken Salad out of Chicken Sh** -Donald Haney

If we are growing we are always going to be outside our comfort zone.

John C. Maxwell

My coach had a saying. He said; you can't make chicken salad out of chicken sh**. That was usually said when a wrestler would ask him if another wrestler was tough or not. It was also posted in our wrestling room. What he was saying if you want to be something in wrestling. Don't be afraid who you are going to battle against. Also, he meant you can't be something without going through something. When he saw his wrestlers were afraid and wrestled like they were afraid, he would say you wrestled like a $3 bill.

When I first heard him say that. I asked a teammate is there such thing as a $3 bill? He looked at me and said. No dummy, what he is saying is that he wrestled like nothing or trash(WOW). From then on, I never wanted to be labeled a $3 bill. When you want to be the best you got to beat the best. If there is no struggle, there is no reward. You're going to have to go through something if you want the best or be best, You noticed on the $3 bill the picture is blocked out.

The reason for that is. If you're going to lay around being afraid to take chances and settle for less to nothing. Take a picture of yourself, and put it in the center of this $3 bill. Because that's what you are.

Wrestlers learn a lot about their opponent, by the handshake at the beginning of the match. Wrestlers know to shake hands with good posture, make eye contact, hold the right hand out, give a good firm shake, follow the two-second rule and smile. You're telling your opponent. You are confident, driven and prepared.

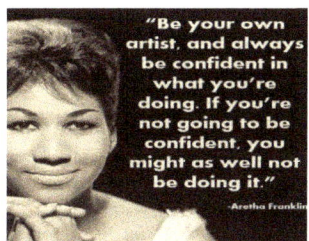

Queen of soul

The easiest thing to do in the world is pulling the covers up over your head and go back to sleep...*Dan Gable*

Right out of high school I never had a fear of getting beaten, which is how most people lose.....*Dan Gable*

Remember your dreams and fight for them ,You must know what you want from LIFE!!!!!

Paulo Coelho

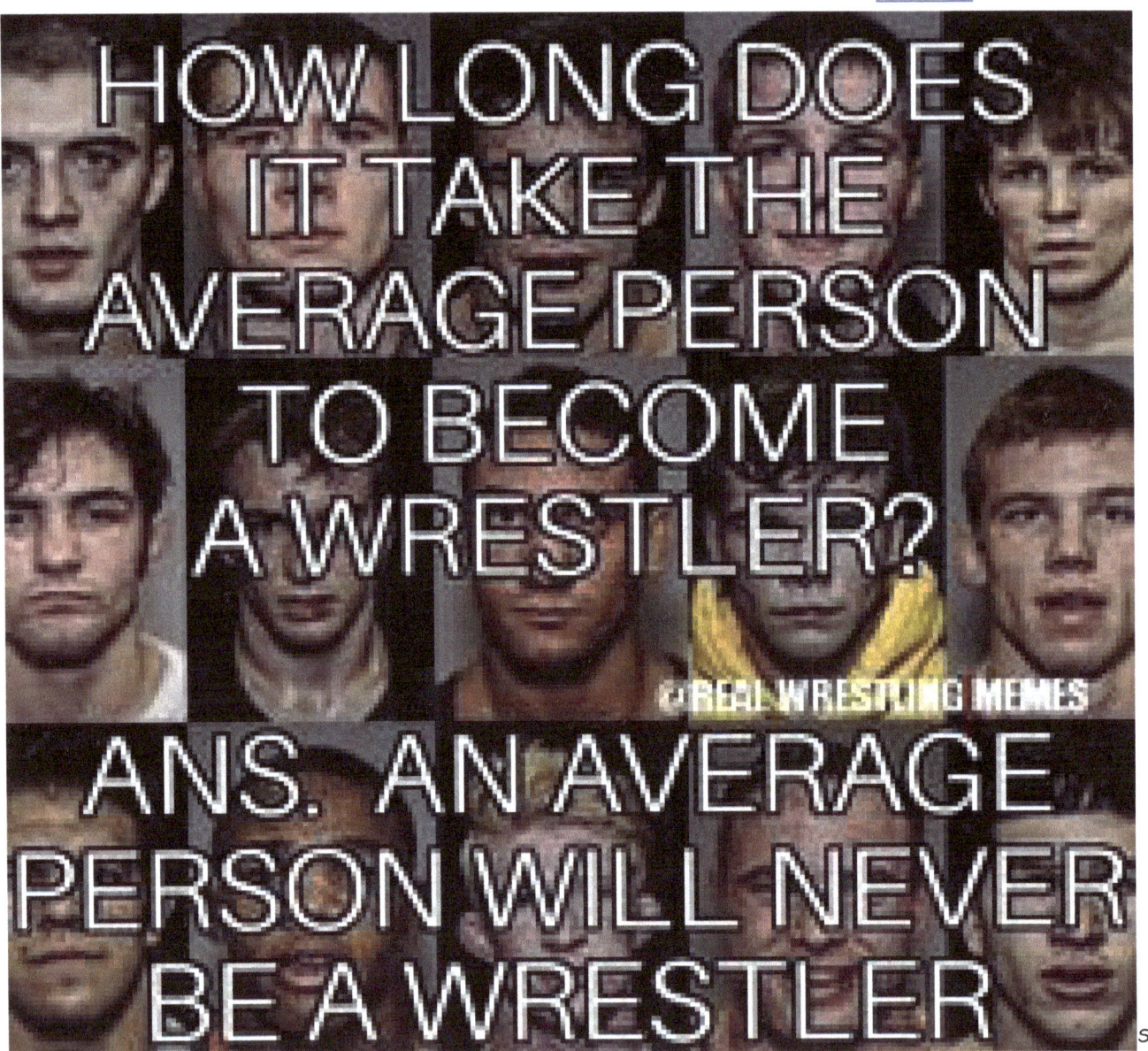

it with the winners, the conversation is different..
Don't be AVERAGE.....

Law #53 in 66 LAWS OF ILLUMINATI...

Never be afraid to try and never be afraid to fail. Go do it, start now, and make it happen and if you fail, **SO WHAT!!!**

Take No-one for granted.....

In wrestling, you're taught never to settle. There is always something you can work on. I wrestled against this guy, who wasn't good at all, I beat him pretty bad, which made me feel really good about myself. When I walked off the mat feeling high and mighty, my coach said to me. You know he pushed you back on your heels at the start of the match? I said yes, what does that have to do with anything? I beat the mess out of him. He said, if that were a top caliber wrestler, that would have been a take-down. Or in others words, he would have scored. That little thing, could be the difference between winning and losing a big match. After he said that to me.

I was like yeah whatever. It just so happen that same day. There was another guy, who was wrestling this guy who wasn't anywhere near his caliber. The lesser guy was getting destroyed. The better wrestler knew he had a guy that wasn't that good at all. So he figured he would have some fun and run the score up on him. At that time in wrestling, you could beat somebody, a hundred to nothing. Now you can only beat somebody by 15 points, then the match automatically stops, which is called a tech fall.

The better wrestler was winning by a great margin. It was like 30 points or more. Pretty much everybody was watching this match in amazement. We all said the same thing. Why doesn't this guy quit and just pin his self? Talking about the Lesser wrestler. Even though he was getting mopped up, the better wrestler couldn't pin the lesser wrestler, because he wouldn't give up. The better wrestler was putting on a show, just doing whatever he wants and laughing and having a good ole time with the lesser wrestler. He went to do a move, tripped and fell on his back, in which the lesser wrestler was able to get on top of him and pin him.

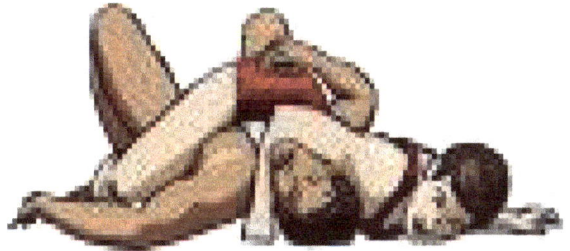

The whole gym erupted. Everybody in the gym, from wrestlers to coaches and parents, were laughing and saying that's what he gets for toying with that guy like that. Everybody congratulated the lesser wrestler for not giving up. My coach seeing that, came to me and said, you see that? I replied, yes I did. I learned after that match. Never give up, no matter how bad it looks. Keep trying, keep pushing yourself. In the end, you will come out ahead. Look pass no one or take anyone for granted.

That match made me work hard every time I got on the mat. I constantly kept pushing myself, till I couldn't push myself anymore, then I pushed even harder. I was in so much fear of that happening to me that I never wanted to wrestle anybody less than me. When I did wrestle somebody less than me. I tried my hardest to put them away early because I to can slip and get pinned by a lesser wrestler.

In life, there's going to be people doing the same thing that you are doing, or trying to have the same achievements as you. People like that will do whatever it takes to get where they want to most likely, in your spot. They will be dedicated; they will put in the hard work, they will be relentless, nothing or no one will stop them.

Even if you see that a person is not as smart as you or as talented as you. Don't overlook that person. When you see a person constantly working hard and dedicating himself to be where you're at. You are going to have to work that much harder. So you can set the bar so high, that no one can reach you. You have to remember. A person who is less than you, in talent and ability will also be hoping that luck is on their side.

The definition of luck is:
When opportunity meets preparation.

Remember back in the wrestling match, when the lesser wrestler was able to take advantage of the opportunity that was giving to him by the better wrestler. The lesser wrestler kept working hard and not giving up which prepared him, for taking the opportunity that was given to him. Which ended in the better wrestler getting pinned and being laughed at. Whatever it is you trying to do or be in life. Always know there is somebody out there doing the same thing as you and looking to knock off, who's ever in their way. Take no one for granted, always figure out ways to do better, even if it's working now. Figure other ways to set yourself apart from the

rest. Remember just like a wrestler. There is something you can always work on.

I fear not the man who has practiced 10,000 kicks once, but I fear the man who has practiced one kick 10,000 times. –*Bruce Lee*

IF, I WISH TEAM..
DON'T BE A MEMBER OF THE WISH I HAD CLUB!

I had a teammate who was a senior and a very good wrestler; sometimes he would skip or miss practice. My coach would ask where is he? I saw him in school today, we would just reply we don't know when we really did know he skipped practice.

My coach had a saying; I never understood to later on. He would say this about him and other wrestlers on the team. He said; they're going to be a part of that IF, I WISH team. I never did understand that and always wondered why he said that. The next year, I found out what he meant by that.

I saw my former teammate who had skip practice and graduated the year previous. We started talking about wrestling and would you believe what he said to me? He said. IF I would have work harder and came to practice, I would be a state champion. I WISH. I would have taken it more seriously. That blew me away. I said to myself; I can't let that happen to me. So every time I stepped on the mat whether in practice or in a match. I worked hard and gave it everything I had. That still sticks with me to this day.

I took, and we all should take from this. When you have a talent no matter what it is. Use it; you have that talent for a reason. When you see an opportunity, don't let fear step in the way,(Limits like Fears are often an illusion -M.J.) take it. If there is something, you want to do in life. Do it, don't worry what other people may say or think.
Fall Forward

If there is something, you want out of life. Go for it. Always do what's best for you. Remember you only have one life to live. You do not want to be in your last days and saying. IF, I WISH. Or even words like I COULDA, I SHOULDA. Making a big life change can be very intimidating and even scary. What's even scarier? **REGRET!!!**

Regrets is a MUTHA.

The bitterest tears shed over graves are for words left unsaid and deeds left undone.

Wall Chart

Life

Wt, <u>Unlimited</u>

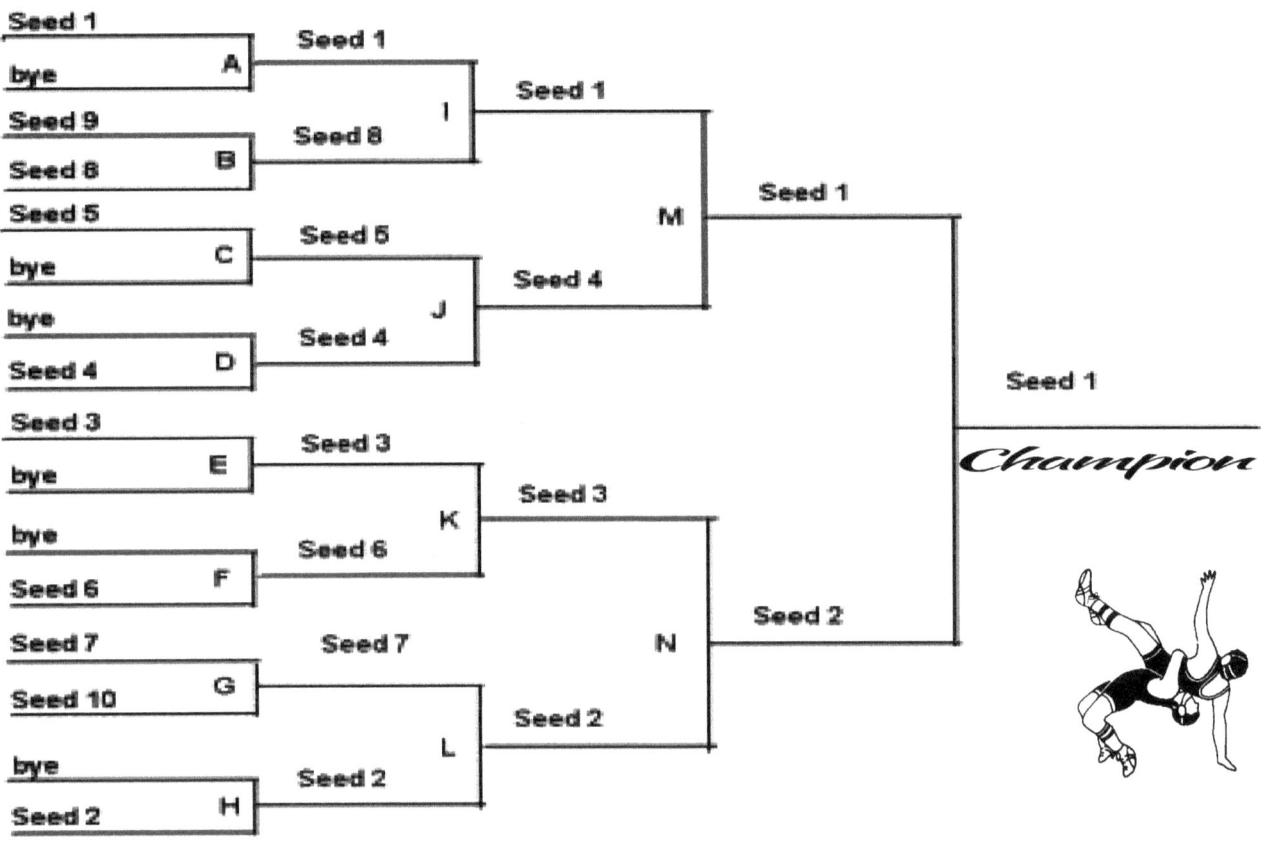

This is a typical wrestling chart, you would see at a tournament. This 16 is a man chart. The best 8 wrestlers are separated from each other. To separated either the day before or two hours before wrestling begins. There is a seating meeting with all the coaches from the different schools in attendance. Coaches vote who should be the top 8 in each weight class, based on their record, head to head competition, wins and losses and just plain common sense. You can see how the wrestlers are separated by the seeds, from 1st to the 8th seed. The majority of the time it ends up the way it is shown here. Some wrestlers can walk through every tournament, being the number 1 seed and winning tournaments with eases. Those are the wrestlers, who have put in hours upon hours of practice to become the best, while as a kid on up to High School, which is now paying off.

In the tournament of life. Some people can handle things and situations like nothing at all. It seems like they got their stuff together and nothing bothers them.

They've learned at an early age how to have faith when facing problems that may arise. This is achieved, by, Parents and family members teachings while growing up, reading self-help books, studying the things they may want to venture into, learning from others mistakes, setting goals, being grateful for what they have, and not focusing on what they don't have, meditating/praying each day, and each day trying to improve in every area of their life.

You see what it takes to be successful in both wrestling and in the match of life. Here is something else you should know.

SUCCESSFUL PEOPLE	UNSUCCESSFUL PEOPLE
Read every day	Watch TV every day
Talk about ideas	Talk about people
Compliment	Complain, criticize
Embrace change	Fear change
Forgive others	Hold grudges
Learn constantly	Are know-it-alls
Accept responsibility for their failures	Blame others for their failures
Have a sense of gratitude	Have a sense of entitlement
Set goals and develop life plans	Never set goals just wing it
Set a budget Save money wisely	Never set a budget Spend money rashly

Which side do you closely relate to. Notice, one side of the list is green. Which means GO!!! or you're going somewhere. The other side is red. Which means STOP!!! or you're going nowhere. Are you on the move? Or are you going nowhere? Wrestlers are aggressive or defensive. Very rare have I seen a defensive wrestler win the big matches. Aggressive wrestlers win big matches, even when the other wrestler is better.

Never be jealous or a hater of anyone, be inspired. We all have the same 24 hours to grind.

Pig-tail/Rat-tail

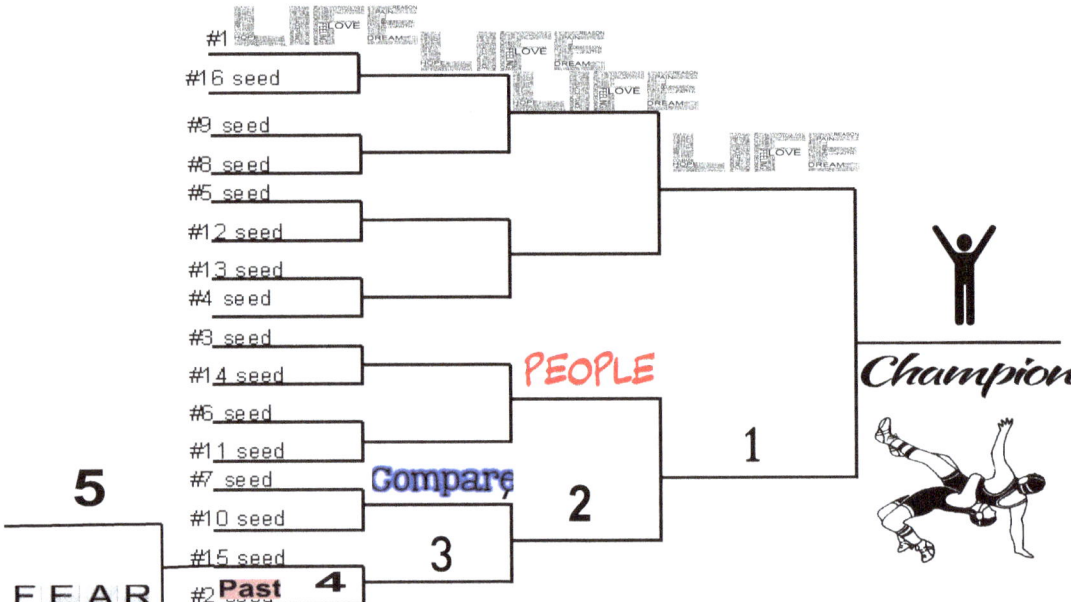

This chart is similar to the other chart. But now you see a little bracket drawn off the back end of the chart. This is known as a rat-tail or pig-tail. It's drawn on a chart if there is someone extra in the weight class. It's usually a person who is not good and could not be seated or even drawn in. This person is basically not in the tournament. They'll have to win a match, just to get in the tournament. If, this person win their rat-tail match. The next match is usually against a person who is a top seed. Then most likely they'll lose that match, which will put them out of the tournament and have to watch from the sidelines the rest of the day.

In the match of life. We to may not be in the tournament. This can happen, due to some poor decision making, insecurities, mistakes, loving the wrong people, trusting the wrong people, no one pushing you to be your best, listening to others on their views of you, the list can go on and on. At one time or another, we all have been out of the tournament and thought what now. It is a must to make up your mind to get in the tournament and not sit on the sidelines watching everyone else succeed. Here are five habits to overcome to succeed in the tournament of life. They are shown and written in different forms and colors. Just like in a wrestling match. Each wrestler is different.

5. Fear:
Don't focus on where you are now, because you will make your now become yours forever. Stop being scared of taking your first step. Instead, gain your power back and trust the process of life. When things were going badly for me. I would say to myself; This time next year I won't be in this situation. Get the right mindset. If you can survive the battles in your mind. You will survive anything. I learned from wrestling, not to give in to fear. Use it as motivation. The best way to eliminate fear is having the right work ethic. Fear of failure leads to failure. Never underestimate the power of thoughts and words. Whatever you tell yourself every morning will set your mind and life on that path. Talk success, victory, happiness, and blessings over your future.

FEAR can keep us up all night long. But **Faith** can make us a fine pillow..

THE PHRASE "DO NOT BE AFRAID" IS WRITTEN IN THE BIBLE 365 TIMES

You can't always control what goes on outside. But you can always control what goes on inside. -Dr. Wayne W. Dyer

4. Past:
The past has no power over the present moment. -Eckhart Tolle

Stop living in your past. Instead, forgive yourself and those who caused you pain and move on. Appreciate where you are in your journey, even if it's not where you want to be. Every season as a purpose.

There's going to be times when you wish you could change some things that happened in the past. There's a reason why the rear-view mirror is so small, and the windshield is so big. Where you're headed is much more important than what you left behind. You should learn, change and grow from your past. When you do those things, you're on the right path. The 3 C's in life: Choice, Chance, Change. You must make the Choice, to take the Chance, if you want anything in life to Change.

3. Comparing:
Stop comparing yourself to others; You'll never feel good enough. Instead, focus on your strengths and let them shine. Don't complain about what's missing. Be grateful for what you already have. When you start comparing yourself to others. You will lose confidence in yourself.

Don't compare with anyone in this world. If you do, you are insulting yourself- *Bill Gates*

2. People:
The people who are worth it will never leave you, so don't grieve over them. It is a blessing in disguise. Cut contact with toxic people. Once you start growing, you will also start cutting. Evaluate the people in your life; Then promote, demote and terminate. You're the CEO of your life. You cannot hang with negative people and expect to live a positive life. When you accept yourself. You are then freed from the burden of needing people to accept you.

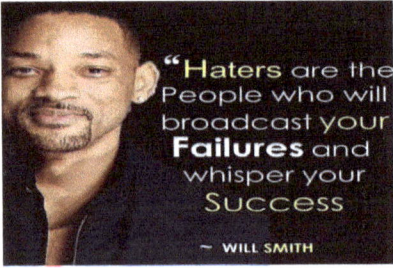

1. Life
Everyone is on a different life journey. Life is not about being rich, being popular, being highly educated or even perfect. Life is about being real, humble, loving and kind. Never lose the drive to learn and live. Somethings will be totally out of your control. You just have to let it go and accept it for what it is. (LIFE!!!!)

Life isn't always fair.

Some people are born into a better environment; some people have better genetics, some are in the right place at the right time. If you're trying to change your life, all of that is irrelevant. All that matters is that you accept where you are.

Figure out where you want to be, then do what you can do today and every day. Hold your head high and keep moving forward. I've coached and seen wrestlers, who were in the rat-tail/pig-tail at the beginning of a tournament. By the end of the tournament, They were champions. Each one was awarded Outstanding Wrestler. Just know. No matter where you're at in this tournament of life. You can be outstanding. Remember that.

Keep moving forward!!!

No matter why things are changing, you have to let go and move on. Whether it's the death of a loved one, a painful breakup, a business failure, or a treacherous betrayal, holding onto past pain and resentment will only hold you back. Life shrinks or expands in proportion to your courage. Even if you fall on your face, you're still moving forward.

Momentum begets momentum, and the best way to start is to start.
Gil Penchina

Life will knock you down many times; it will show you things you never wanted to see. You will experience sadness and failures. One thing is always for sure. You can always get up. The law of life is the law of belief. A belief is a thought in your mind. Always believe in the power of your subconscious for healing, to inspire, to strengthen and for prosperity.

Note: Most people don't believe what they see. They rather see what they have already decided to believe.-Universal Believe

Hebrew 11:1-NIV
Now faith is confidence in what we hope for and assurance about what we do not see.

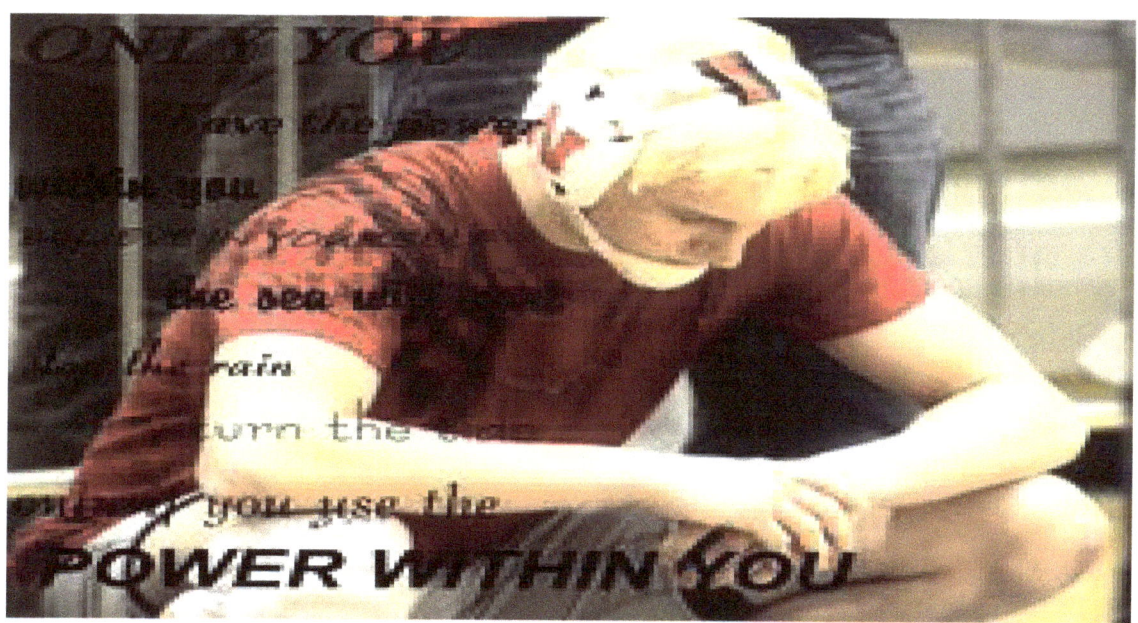

STRESSED?

Jeremiah 29:11
"For I know the thoughts that I think toward you, saith the LORD, thoughts of peace, and not of evil, to give you an expected end."

Proverbs 29:11
"A fool uttereth all his mind: but a wise man keepeth it in till afterwards."

Proverbs 3:5-6
"Trust in the LORD with all thine heart; and lean not unto thine own understanding. In all thy ways acknowledge him, and he shall direct thy paths."

Ephesians 4:26
"Be ye angry, and sin not: let not the sun go down upon your wrath."

Ephesians 4:31-32
"Let all bitterness, and wrath, and anger, and clamour, and evil speaking, be put away from you, with all malice. And be ye kind one to another, tenderhearted, forgiving one another, even as God for Christ's sake hath forgiven you."

Matthew 6:19-21
"Lay not up for yourselves treasures upon earth, where moth and rust doth corrupt, and where thieves break through and steal: But lay up for yourselves treasures in heaven, where neither moth nor rust doth corrupt, and where thieves do not break through nor steal: For where your treasure is, there will your heart be also."

Romans 8:28
"And we know that all things work together for good to them that love God, to them who are the called according to his purpose."

Hebrews 12:6
"For whom the Lord loveth he chasteneth, and scourgeth every son he receiveth."

Starting Over...

Wrestling my last year in junior high school, I was undefeated with a record of 20 wins 0 losses 1 tie. I went on to be an All-City champion. I just knew I was the stuff(sh**) nobody could touch me or tell me anything. I got to high school. All that went out the window. On my first day of practice. I got my butt(a**) kicked. Every move I used in junior high, didn't work at all. I was getting thrown around like nothing. I can't count how many times I got pinned. I got put into holes, where I almost wanted to cry.

Besides getting my a** kicked, the conditioning was even harder than the junior high. After crawling up the stairs after practice. I went home, got my All City Championship chart and medal. I ripped up the chart and threw it and the medal in the trash. I knew from then on. What I did in junior high was nothing, and I'll have to start all over again in High School. It took me a little while to get the whole understanding and Logistics of wrestling on the next level. I did get it and became successful. Other guys that wrestled with me in Jr High could not make the transition or didn't want to. So they quit, and their wrestling career was over.

There going to be many times you have to start over. The way you have gone about and did things before, are not working now. So you have to relearn, educate, practice and study. That's just a fact of life; nothing stays the same.

You must be willing to change with the times and new situations. After 20 years of coaching wrestling. I retired because I wasn't willing to change with the times. Wrestling was starting to pass me by. I had got older and still had the old-school way of wrestling. I was noticing that my way wasn't working, and I wasn't willing to relearn, re-educate, practice or study the new way of wrestling. So I retired. You also may have to get out of certain relationships. It can be friends, relatives, and even spouses.

We all come to a point in our life, Where we are going to start over. Not everyone is going to want to start over or make a change with you. You have to separate yourself from them. You don't need someone to hinder or hold you back from the things you want in life. Don't waste time on those people. Time is something you never get back.

Starting over or making a change, isn't always a bad thing. As long as you are starting over or changing for a better you and a brighter future.

Failure is the opportunity to start over again more intelligently...........

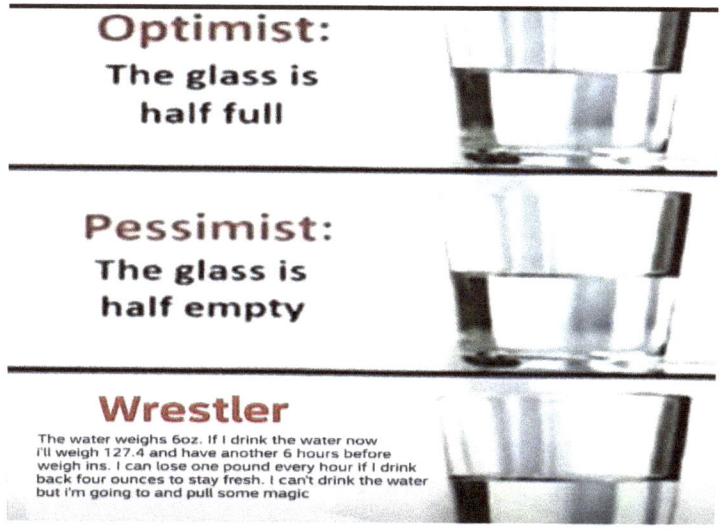

Have the mind of a wrestler.

Excuses...

Excuses are the nails used to build a house of failure.

For all their bitching about what's holding them back, most people have a lot of trouble coming up with the defined dreams they're being held from. -Tim Ferriss

[Anthony Robles](#) is a wrestler who is born with only one leg. Refusing to wear a prosthetic leg, removing it at the age of 3. With no leg up to his hip, without stump to attach a prosthetic leg. He works around his missing leg, strengthening his body with various exercises. In sixth grade, he set a record for the most pushups. He started wrestling in Jr high; In 9th grade, he had a record of 5–8. Being always 10 pounds under his weight class. He never cut weight. Not giving up on wrestling. He learned how to use his low center of gravity. Which he created many moves. He graduated from High School with 129 wins, 15 loses 2 state championships and a High School national championship.

With those great achievements. Not one big wrestling college want him. He started his college wrestling career at Arizona State University. With the many challenges, he faced, wrestling on the division 1 level. Which isn't easy for a wrestler with two arms and two legs. Anthony worked his way to 122 wins,23 loses, with three PAC-10 titles, three-time All-American and graduated as a national champion.

Definition of the word Excuse:
Attempt to lessen the blame attaching to (a fault or offense); seek to defend or justify.

This wrestler had every excuse to give up on life. I'm sure the kids in school wasn't nice at all, by teasing and saying bad things. I would say, he sat at home and cried many times. Most would say he was giving a raw deal. Why would God do this to him?

All the great wrestlers that ever stepped on a wrestling mat will tell you. Nothing's going to stop them from achieving their goal. All top wrestlers focus, is to be a State Champion, National Champion, World Champion, and Olympic Champion. They make unbelievable sacrifices to achieve these high goals. They believe, as long as there is air in their lungs. They can have whatever they want on the mat and off the mat.

Wrestler's don't believe in the words; handicap, can't, fail, looser, less and unskilled. Over the years as a coach. I have come across many individuals. Who have two arms two legs, healthy, strong and of sound mind. Most just wanted to have a winning record, place in tournaments and get a varsity letter. I would tell them you can have so much more than that. You just have to put in the work and have the right mindset. I would say you need to change your thinking. I let them know they're cheating themselves of great rewards. They would tell me, They're not very athletic, not strong enough and have no talent. I would say back to them. SO WHAT!!!!

You just have to want it and work even harder and good things will come your way. They would reply; that's okay. People I've met in my life travels, who were also in perfect health with all their limbs. Would say to me; all they want out of life. A good job, a nice house, a nice car, a good spouse, healthy kids, be able to go to work every day and then retire. I would say to them that's good to want that, but there is so much more you can have out of life if you choose. Their reply is; I'm content.

Then there are those, who say they can't get ahead because society is holding them back, their skin color, nobody wants to see them get ahead, that sounds like work, cost too much, I don't have a car, I'm broke, they don't pay enough, don't have the right clothes, that's too early to get up, I'll try something else, I like hanging out too much. That's just some of the excuses I've heard. When I would say; you can do certain things to better yourself and your life.

Your excuses are nothing more than the lies your fears have sold you.-Robin Sharma

If you say, you can do something, or you say you can't do something, you're right.-Henry Ford

It's amazing, seeing a person born with a handicap, who is getting far in life and having a very fulfilled and successful life. Then seeing people who are perfectly healthy. Who are just content to be where they are at or just don't want to put in the work to have a great life. We all have choices. Choose wisely; you don't want to get to the end and look back with regrets.

I heard a person speak once. He said; Imagine you're on your death bed. With everything around you, that you could have done or achieved when you were young and healthy but made an excuse why you can't. Just think, It's too late.

Facts: An excuse is nothing more than a self-imposed roadblock.
If it is important to you, you will find a way. If not you will find an excuse.

Difficulty is the excuse history never accepts.

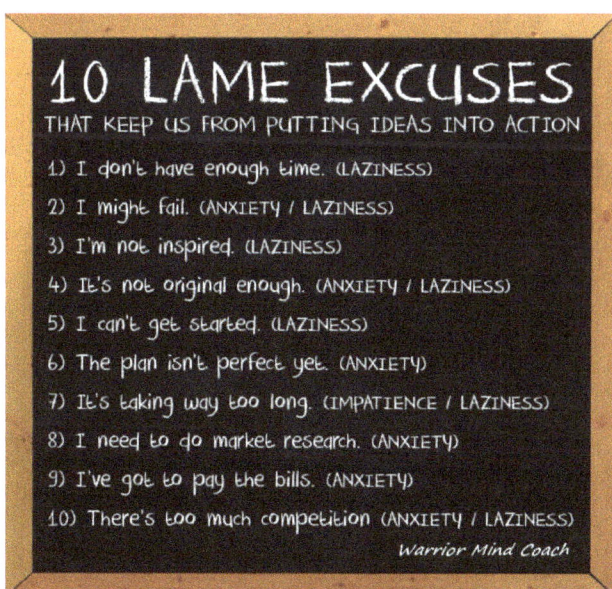

Laziness is a dangerous thing. It will destroy you if you don't destroy it.....

Ask yourself how badly do **YOU** want it?

> "One day, you will wake up and there won't be any more time to do the things you've always wanted. Do it now."
>
> — Paulo Coelho

Law #58 in 66 LAWS OF ILLUMINATI...

Provide no excuses, give an explanation only if required, but do offer an apology if the fault error is found to be yours...

Till I became one...

I grew up thinking that wrestling was some guys wearing speedo's, jumping off ropes, hitting each other with chairs and doing pile drivers, until I became a wrestler. There were times when I thought my coaches, was just being outright mean. Making myself and teammates do all this extra stuff, I believed to be unnecessary. I would get very upset with them. I'd believed they were just having us do extra because they had the power over us. When I became a coach, I started doing the same things that my coaches in the past had done; now I knew why they were doing it.

As a coach. I believed the referees, were just plain bad and always had it out for me and my wrestlers. I was wrong again. When I became a referee, I started seeing things, that coaches didn't see or thought was wrong. It took me becoming a ref, to see what they go through. I definitely have a different perspective on referees.

People are going to judge you for the things you have done in your past, and the things you are currently doing without knowing anything about you and your situation. Majority of the people who are saying what you should be and not be doing. Are not walking in your shoes, have not been through what you have been through and not trying to help you. They're quick to have an opinion or pass judgment.

Matthew 7:1-5 says:

Do not judge, or you too will be judged. 2 For in the same way you judge others, you will be judged, and with the measure you use, it will be measured to you. 3 "Why do you look at the speck of sawdust in your brother's eye and pay no attention to the plank in your own eye? 4 How can you say to your brother, 'Let me take the speck out of your eye,' when all the time there is a plank in your own eye? 5 You hypocrite, first take the plank out of your own eye, and then you will see clearly to remove the speck from your brother's eye.

Laws of Attraction:

Don't be so Quick to judge, you never know when you might just find yourself walking in that person's shoes.

People are so quick to judge and make decisions for themselves, about situations they know absolutely nothing about.

Don't judge what you don't understand.

Those who judge will never understand, and those who understand will never judge.
People are quick to judge a book by the chapter they came in on.
People will attack what they don't understand. Most people who are saying things to you, about you and passing judgment on you, have not walked in your shoes.

Those are the ones you stay away from and don't listen to. The people who have been through what you're going through will not say things or judge you. They're going to help you. Stay away from so call friends, relatives, and even spouses if they are not helping or lifting you to better yourself.

Wrestlers don't practice with anybody, who cannot make them better or understand certain problems they may have on the mat. They only want those who been there and understand the problems and situations. You will have to do the same, even in life.

Don't be in such a hurry to condemn a person because he doesn't do what you do, or think as you think. There was a time when you didn't know what you know today.- Malcolm X

This is you. Let nothing or no one stop you. Wrestlers are taught to be a beast on the mat. You can be a beast in life. Just like a wrestler.

3rd Period

Always be a first-rate version of yourself, instead of a second-rate version of somebody else.

Judy Garland

Instant Karma...

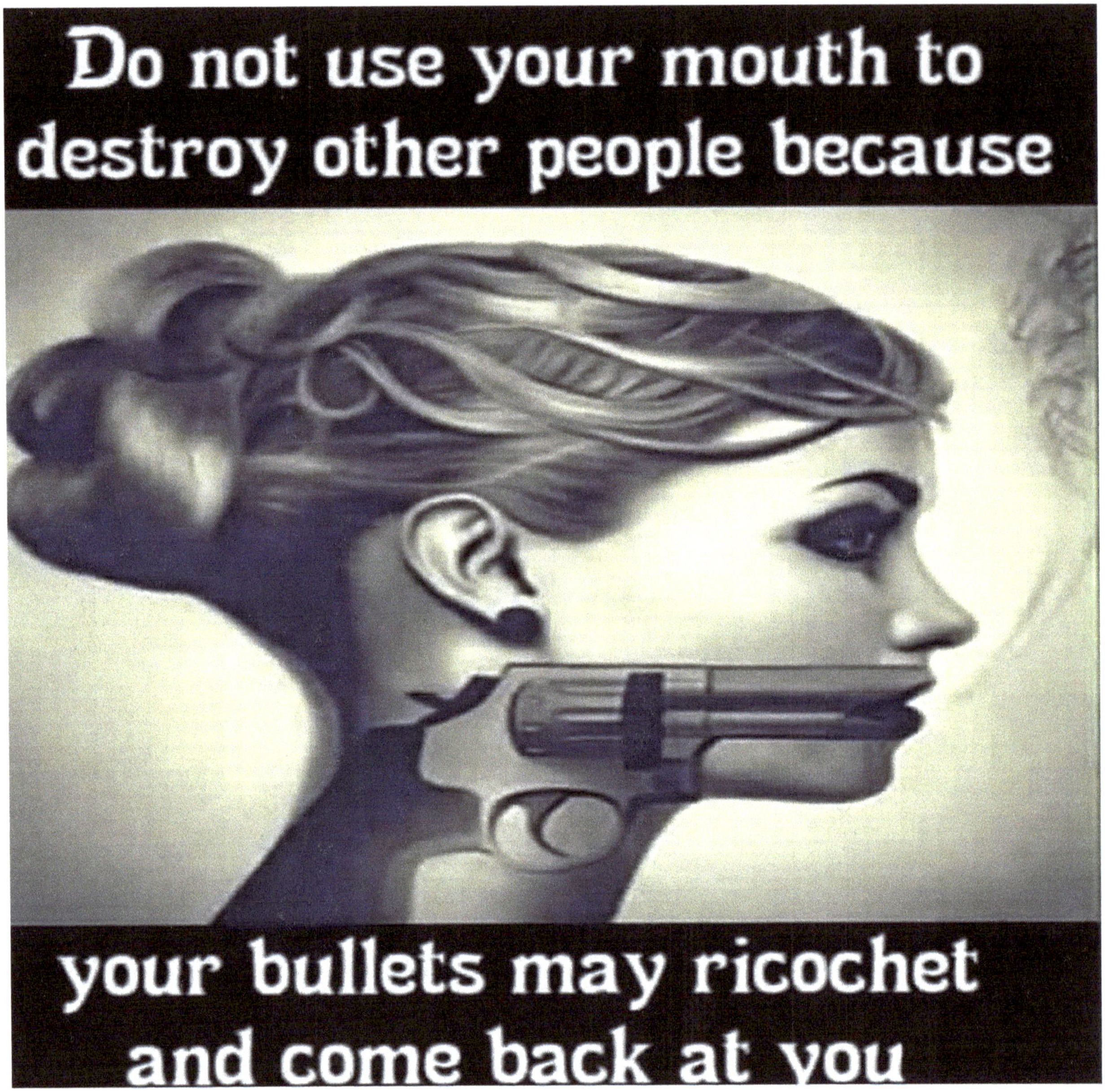

Do not use your mouth to destroy other people because
your bullets may ricochet and come back at you

$+$

$=$

BANG!

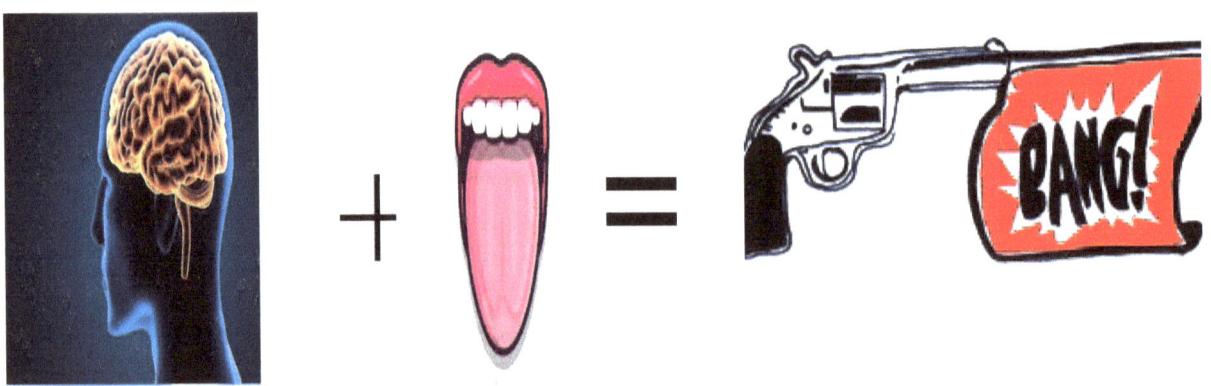

The tongue is a small thing., but it can do major damage.

Galatians: 6:7

A man reaps what he sows. You will always harvest what you plant.

Hinduism, Buddhism:

Action seen as bringing upon oneself inevitable results, good or bad, either in this life or in a reincarnation.

Theosophy:

The cosmic principle according to which each person is rewarded or punished in one incarnation according to that person's deeds in the previous incarnation.

Life echo's what you give out. What you sow, You reap. What you give, You get. What you see in others, Exists in you. Remember, life is an echo. It always gets back to YOU.

One day, just before practice was to start. I saw some of my teammates, teasing another teammate who wasn't a very good wrestler. They were saying how bad he is, how he would never have a winning record, he would be lucky if you score a point in a match, he would never make the varsity line-up. They were just letting him know how plain sorry he is. I joined in also, telling him how bad he is. He replied to me saying that he would take me down. Now mind you, I could beat him with one arm tied behind my back, he was no match for me at all. "When," he said that to me. I replied saying;

You will never score on me a day in your life!!!!!!!!!!

A day, happened to be that day. As practice was coming to an end, my coach asked is there anyone who wants to go an extra match, step on the mat. I stepped on the mat, guess who stepped across from me. You guessed it. The very one I said, wouldn't score on me a day in his life. No one else on the team wanted to go an extra match. That left him and I on the mat, or you can say in the spotlight. I remember thinking to myself this will be easy just get some conditioning and maybe try some new moves.

My coach blew the whistle he shot in for my legs. I did a move called a sprawl; it's when you throw your legs back and make it hard for your opponent to grab them. He normally flattens out when I do that. I go around to score a take-down, this time, he didn't flatten out. He had a hold of my legs, picked me way up in the air and slammed me on my head, not only did he score he made me look a awful fool. Everybody in the wrestling room was laughing very hard including my coaches. He even said; I thought I was never going to score on you. **TAKE THAT!!!!!!** After he said that. I went on to destroy him and pin him, but the damage was done.

After practice in the locker room. He and the other teammates were still talking about that. They continued making fun of me and laughing in my face, saying you must not be that good. He dropped you on your head; he was saying yeah must not be.

He was in his glory, to make things even worst. The next day in school right as I walked into the school, people came to me saying, I heard you got dropped on your head by him. I couldn't believe how something like that spread so fast. This went on for a very long time.

You would have thought it would have stopped in high school. It did not. I saw him at our 20-year class reunion. Besides telling me how he's living his life. He reminded me of that day 20 years prior. He went on to say, every time the subject of wrestling comes up. He tells people how he dropped one of the best wrestlers in the state on his head, then stood over him and said, Take that. As he was telling me this. He swoll up, balled his fists and stuck his chest out. I was thinking to myself. What I said, really had affected him. The rest of that night, after he got drunk, everytime he saw me or walk near where I was at. He would stick his chest out, ball his fist, growl at me and say **TAKE THAT!!!!!!**. This shows how one person affects another person.

When I look back on that whole situation. I should have told my teammates to stop talking about him. I should have said, at least he comes to practice every day, gives his all. I should have pulled him aside, worked with him to make him a better wrestler. This would have made him feel important and thought of me, more positively.

When I became a coach. The kids who weren't very talented or not really good but came to practice and gave it their all every-day. I made it my duty to work with them and encourage them every chance I got. I always made them feel special and important. Just talking to them made them feel like they were somebody and special. I remember hearing one of my wrestlers telling his teammate after he won his match. He said. I must have done good because coach said I did well. Referring to me.

I got sick where I had to stay in the hospital. The other coaches told me how the kids were worried about me and wanted to come to see me in the hospital. That made me feel really good. I know they felt that way, because of the way, I treated them. When I came back to practice after being in the hospital. They were glad to see me and gave me a get well card.

Bottom-line. Treat people with love and kindness. Or as the old saying goes; treat people how you wanna be treated. It doesn't take much to make another person day bright. A smile and a handshake can do wonders. Remember karma ain't a joke. It also has no time limit. People forget the things you may have done for them. People will always remember how you made them feel.

KARMA IS THE BIGGEST GANG$TER KNOWN TO MAN.

Know This:
When a bird is alive, it eats ants. When the bird die, ants eat it. Circumstances(Things) can change in an instant. Don't put down or hurt anyone in this life. You may be powerful today but time is more powerful than **YOU!!!**

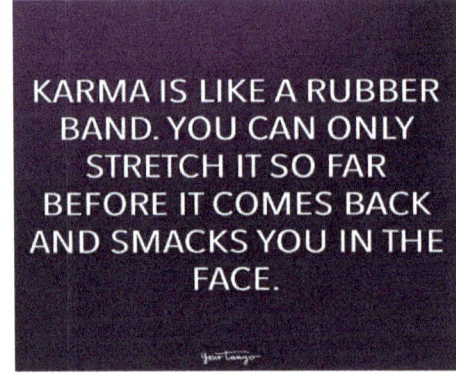

If someone hurts you...

Law #33 in 66 LAWS OF ILLUMINATI...

Revenge will destroy the light and weaken the family. Revenge should always be avoided but if it come down to it, then revenge must be balanced with justice. But in the house of illuminati, the only revenge is **SUCCESS!!!**

LESSON 33: Revenge dampens your light because it causes you to focus on things which make no contribution to your success. Repay a wrong with kindness. Show love to your enemies and it will eat them up. Love is the only revenge that you will need. Illuminati is not concerned with revenge, only success. Be just in all your actions. Although ancient leaders warned that if you leave your enemy standing, he will return to destroy you.

Illuminati does not support such actions. Always use the light and wisdom to avoid war and revenge. Matter of fact, the only true revenge is for you to succeed in your goals.

When an enemy wants you to fail, then the most long-lasting revenge is for you to rise to higher heights, prevail against the odds, and achieve success in whatever your goals!

Stick it to your enemy by being successful. Imagine the sting when you achieve in spite of all odds...

Sharing O.J.

There is a saying at the school, I wrestled for and coached. The saying is; sharing O.J. It is said when you or your teammate is talking and being friendly to wrestlers from other schools. "When" we would see that. We would say to our teammate; there you go sharing O.J. Save me some O.J.

Wrestlers from the other schools had no clue what we were talking about, especially if there was no orange juice around. "When" I was told how this saying came about. I thought it was pretty funny. A former wrestler from my school, who is a two-time all-state wrestler, would sit in the bleachers with wrestlers from other schools, most of whom he had to wrestle against. He would share his orange juice with them. His teammates would see him doing that, they would say; there he goes sharing O.J. The funny part about that is. Even though he would share his orange juice with them, he would wrestle them and beat the crap out of them. It was like he took their guard down.

As" a coach. I had a wrestler who took sharing o j, to a whole different level. He didn't share orange juice but showed his opponent, he is to wrestle against. The wrestling moves that he uses to win matches. The very move he showed him was used by his opponent to beat him.

What's learned from these two wrestlers. Whatever you are trying to do or achieve, and somebody else is trying to do the same things as you. Never let them know your plans or idea's because it may just get used to defeat you.

Make people think you are one way, and come to find out you are totally opposite of that. Which will shock them and not know what to do or think. Wrestlers keep their best moves hid; they know other opponents are watching.
In the book [48 Laws of Power](#). There are certain laws to go by, to control a rival.

LAW 14

POSE AS A FRIEND, WORK AS A SPY

Knowing about your rival is critical. Use spies to gather valuable information that will keep you a step ahead. Better still: Play the spy yourself. In polite social encounters, learn to probe. Ask indirect questions to get people to reveal their weaknesses and intentions. No occasion is not an opportunity for artful spying.

LAW 15

CRUSH YOUR ENEMY TOTALLY

All great leaders since Moses have known that a feared enemy must be crushed completely. (Sometimes they have learned this the hard way.) If one ember is left alight, no matter how dimly it smolders, a fire will eventually break out. More is lost through stopping halfway than through total annihilation: the enemy will recover and will seek revenge. Crush him, not only in body but in spirit.

LAW 17

CULTIVATE AN AIR OF UNPREDICTABILITY

Humans are creatures of habit with an insatiable need to see familiarity in other people's actions. Your predictability gives them a sense of control. Turn the tables: be deliberately unpredictable. Behavior that seems to have no consistency or purpose will keep them off balance, and they will wear themselves out trying to explain your moves. Taken to an extreme, this strategy can intimidate and terrorize.

LAW 21

SEEM DUMBER THAN YOUR MARK

No one likes feeling stupider than the next person. The trick is to make your victims feel smart - and not just smart, but smarter than you are. Once convinced of this, they will never suspect that you may have ulterior motives.

Wrestlers live by these laws. You can also.

Never be a person who shares O.J.

Law #19 in 66 LAWS OF ILLUMINATI...

What happens in the House of Illuminati, stays in the House of Illuminati. Keep the business of the light to yourself and only the brothers and sisters of the light...

House business is only meant for those in the House. What goes on in the House stays in the House. Don't share everything with everyone. Don't put all your business in the streets. Guard what is secret and protect what is sacred.

Be careful who you tell your business because everyone does not have your best interest in mind. Some things may be used against you at a later date. Be selective in what you share and think twice before you speak. Either find a trust-worthy confidant or share with those who already now...

The 48 Laws of Power

1 Never outshine the master	9 Win through actions, never through argument	17 Keep others in suspended terror: Cultivate an air of unpredictability	25 Re-create yourself	33 Discover each man's thumbscrew	41 Avoid stepping in to a great man's shoes
2 Never put too much trust in friends, learn how to use enemies	10 Infection: Avoid the unhappy an unlucky	18 Do not build fortresses to protect yourself - Isolation is dangerous	26 Keep your hands clean	34 Be royal in your on fashion: Act like a king to be treated like one	42 Strike the shepherd and the sheep will scatter
3 Conceal your intentions	11 Learn to keep people dependent on you	19 Know who you're dealing with – Do not offend the wrong person	27 Play on people's needs to believe to create a cult-like following	35 Master the art of timing	43 Work on the hearts and minds of others
4 Always say less than necessary	12 Use selective honesty and generosity to disarm your victim	20 Do not commit to anyone	28 Enter action with boldness	36 Misdain things you cannot have: Ignoring them is the best revenge	44 Disarm and infuriate with the mirror effect
5 So much depends on reputation – Guard it with your life	13 When asking for help, appeal to people's self-interest, never to their mercy or gratitude	21 Play a sucker to catch a sucker – Seem dumber than your mark	29 Plan all the way to the end	37 Create compelling spectacles	45 Preach the need for change, but never reform too much at once
6 Court attention at all cost	14 Pose as a friend, work as as spy	22 Use surrender tactic: Transform weakness into power	30 Make your accomplishments seem effortless	38 Think as you like but behave like others	46 Never appear too perfect
7 Get others to do the work for you, but always take the credit	15 Crush your enemy totally	23 Concentrate your forces	31 Control the options: Get others to play with the cards you deal	39 Stir up waters to catch fish	47 Do not go past the mark you aimed for; In victory, learn when to stop
8 Make other people come to you, use bait if necessary	16 Use absence to increase respect and honor	24 Play the perfect courtier	32 Play to people's fantasies	40 Despise the free lunch	48 Assume formlessness

High level...

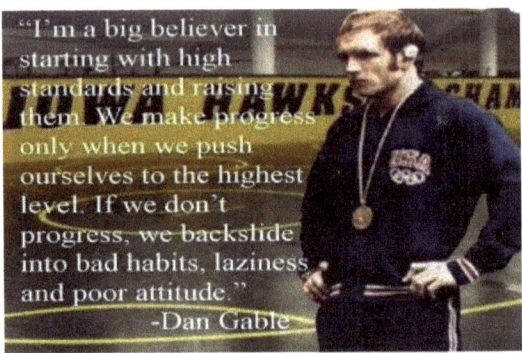

My last year in high school. I needed a place to workout before the actual season started. At the time we didn't have a coach or knew who was going to be the coach. I was told about this one school who was having preseason workouts. Actually, I didn't even know this school had a team. I never read about them or even heard about them in wrestling.

I contacted the wrestling coach at the school and was allowed to go there and work out with the guys on the team. Needless to say. I see why I hadn't heard of this school having a wrestling team or anyone wrestling for this school. These guys were outright horrible. From day one I was destroying them.

I could beat everybody on the team, from lightweight to heavyweight and even the coach. I practice with them three days a week. I would toy with them and have my way any time I wanted. This went on for a good month. Till one day, I notice. The same guys I was having my way with, started to stick with me. Slowly and slowly I started having troubles beating them. It got to the point to where I couldn't show-off, talk junk while wrestling them, or even take a breather while wrestling them.

At one practice a guy I always had my way with, gave me all I could handle. But I pulled the match out, right at the end. That just built up his confidence. Then he started talking trash. He was saying. You ain't all that, the next time we wrestle I'm going to beat you. Right then and there I realized something. These guys didn't get better. I had come down to their level. Which was a low-level in wrestling? After that day. I never practice with them again, because they actually brought me down to their level of wrestling.

I couldn't wait to get back to wrestling my own teammate, who gave me fits and I had to work for everything. We all kept each other on a high level. The guy I wrestled in the state finals, was the best wrestler on his team. He didn't practice with his teammates; he went to the local college practices so that he would stay at a high level.

In wrestling, there is such a thing called a good loss. That's when you go against one of the top guys and lose a close match to him. A wrestler should always want to wrestle the top guy in his weight. That way he can gauge how good he is, and if he can beat the top guys in his weight.

If you a lose close match to him. That's actually a good thing. Now you can see where you measure up with the top guys out there. Plus you can see what you need to work on to get better, and reach their level and pass them.

In life, when you are deciding on a mate. One of the things you should always look for. Is this person going to lift you to reach higher levels in life? Can this person help you reach your goals, is this person going to keep you on the same level, or bring you down from where you are already at in life.

When you are trying to reach a certain goal or start a business. Make sure to get people around you, who are smarter than you or who have already achieved great success at what you're trying to do. Remember the best way to look smart, is to have smart people around you.

If you're the smartest one in your group, you need a new group. If you are good and very smart at something, make sure you are inspiring the surrounding people to be even better than you. This will turn into a win-win situation. When you lose or fail, because you went against something or someone who is better at the same thing you are trying to do or achieve. Make sure you learn from this failure.

Always seek what it is you did wrong, so the next time you will be well-equipped and ready the next time.

Wrestlers always see the score as 0 to 0. This will constantly, make them wrestle as hard as they can, to win the match. Aways do your best to stay at a high level in whatever it is you want or trying to do in life. You only have one life to live. No one else can live it for you, so do whatever it takes to rise above all.

When you achieve the goals and dreams, you wanted for your life. Don't worry what people will say, no matter who's saying the negative things about you. When you want rain, you have to deal with the mud. People see your destination, not your journey. Always imagine yourself as a Champion.

Dream big. Start small. Act now-Robin Sharma

YOU EARN YOUR TROPHIES AT PRACTICE. YOU JUST PICK THEM UP AT COMPETITIONS.

WE ARE.

The person we believe ourselves to be will always act in a manner consistent with our self-image.- Brian Tracy

There's a prestigious High School, here in Michigan. Whose name I can't say. But if you're from my area, you know exactly the school I'm talking about. The parents own big companies; others are doctors, lawyers, professors, own lots of properties. A new school was built on the property donated by an alumni of the school. I can't begin to describe this new school. Let's just say **amazing.** If you are a student at this school. You will get the very best education.

When you are not a part of the school in any way. You're considered beneath them. Rarely associating with anyone not associated with the school. This school is very good at all their sports programs. Their wrestling team is one of the top teams in the country. At the writing of this book. Their wrestling team has been in the state finals 7 times and winning six championships. If you don't know the sport of wrestling and came across either the coaches or wrestlers. You would say they're arrogant.

Neither the coaches nor wrestlers say much to anyone not associated with the school. The wrestling does the talking for them. This is very intimidating. Remember as I said before. (The 1st rule in laws of Power. If you want to control someone. Say nothing at all). This is how a wrestler should carry himself. Which this school does a great job of it.

Now there's another High School here in Michigan. Again whose name I cannot say. This High School is the total opposite, of the school I just told you about. These parents work regular manufacturing, construction, and production jobs; most work two jobs to make ends meet. The school is rather old with some updates, but nowhere near in comparison to the other school, I just described.

You can receive a fair education from this school, but not like the other school. The majority of their Sports programs are not good at all. They haven't had a winning wrestling team in many years. In fact, the wrestling program is in danger of being dropped from the school. The wrestlers on the team are not intimidating at all. Simply because they're not that good and not trying to be good. The last time this school has done anything great in wrestling. I was barely alive.

Even though these two schools and everything associated with these two schools, are the total opposite. They do have something in common. They both have a saying. The saying is; **WE ARE!!!!** Everybody associated with the first school will let you know who they are. The school has one cheer that says; WE ARE(school name). After "we are" is said, then the school name is said. Which for them, means respect us and the name. Because of the way they carry themselves and let it be known who they are. Everybody gives them total respect. When others talk about this school. It's in total respect.

The other school, when **WE ARE!!!!** is said. It signifies we suck and will always suck. A lot of the kids associated with the school will tell you themselves WE ARE(school name). Which means don't expect anything good from us? Because of the way they carry themselves and what they believe of themselves. They are treated with total disrespect on and off the mat.

Both schools are treated the same way they treat themselves. Always remember however you see yourself and how you carry yourself. You will be treated the same way by others. If you think you're not that good-looking and carry yourself like you're not good-looking, people will see you as ugly.

If you're not as attractive as others, but carry yourself like you're the most beautiful person in the world. People will come to believe and say you are attractive. Always carry yourself in a positive manner. Never let people treat you negatively. If you do, you're allowing people to disrespect you. Respect is earned not given. Always love yourself the way you love someone else.

Proverbs 4:23
Carefully guard your thoughts because they are the source of true life

All that we are is a result of what we have thought. - *Buddha*

Never accept anything less than you deserve. Remember, you teach people how to treat you...

When I was 9, I saw a wrestler on television named Gorgeous George. He said I'm beautiful. I'm so pretty that if a sucker touches my face. I'll kill him. If he messes with my hair. I'll pummel him. I said to myself. That's a good idea. I am the greatest, I'm pretty, and then I took it a little further than he did.

"I am the greatest. I said that even before I knew I was. I figured that if I said it enough, I would convince the world that I really was the greatest

To be a great champion, you must believe you are the best. If you're not, pretend you are.-Muhammad Ali

MY ALL-TIME FAVORITE ATHLETE.

THE GREATEST OF ALL TIME

G.O.A.T

You can be a G.O.A.T. Just believe in you.

Don't wait for the world to recognize your greatness, live it and let the world catch up to you.

Vision

I'm a big believer in dreaming. If you don't dream it, you can't become it-Magic Johnson

Make your vision so clear that your fears become irrelevant.

Your awareness and focus on a subject is creating your experience in reality..

A person without vision for the future, always returns to the past..

If you want to get better. It is best to work on your moves over and over and over and over, till you dream about them, and then you work on them some more this is called Drilling. I was taught drill, drill, drill, drill, drill, till you can't drill anymore, then start drilling again. This is the number one way to become a great wrestler. You have to be able to do the moves without even thinking about them.

The moves have to be ingrained in your head and muscles. There is another way to learn moves and have them ingrained in your whole being. Seeing someone else do a move whether in practice or in a match. Most wrestlers called this; a vision. The see's someone else wrestling. Then see the move that they're doing, then vision themselves doing the move they saw. It happens all the time. I can't tell you how many times it has happened to me, teammates and kids I've coached. I would ask the teammates and the kids I coached. I have never seen you do that move before, where did that come from? I always got the same reply. I saw someone else doing it, I just vision myself doing it, and I did it.

I was watching the NCAA wrestling championships. There was a guy who won the national championship as a true freshman. The announcers knew him very well. The announcer said one of the things that this wrestler would do is watch videos of great wrestlers from the past. This particular wrestler would spend hours and hours watching all the great wrestlers videos. He would do this every day. The announcer said by him seeing the other greats wrestling moves he was doing them himself.

This is what helped him to be a national champion as a true freshman. After he won the national championship, the wrestler was interviewed. He was asked how does it feel to be a national champion? The wrestler said it feels great, but I already knew I was going to be a national champion because I visioned it.

Whatever it is you want in life or out of life. You have to put the work into it over and over and over until it totally consumes you. While you're working very hard to achieve what you want. Have a vision of how you want your life to be. Ask a successful person how doe's his life look a year from now. He would be able to tell you. Because he visioned it.

A non-successful person wouldn't be able to tell you. Because they have no vision. See yourself doing it. Create what is called a vision board. It's a picture of everything you want out of life. A board for you to see every day. Look at it every day and vision what your future will be. It has been said and is true what you see in your mind you can in your hand. It's called the law of attraction. I'm sure most of you reading this book, have done this and just didn't know it.

I was able to see what I wanted to do, I could see the opportunity, even when others could not, and I stay committed to doing it and doing it well, no matter what. -*Magic Johnson*

Wrestling Vision Board

Life Vision Board

There are many ways of motivating yourself to higher levels. Write about it, dream about it. But after that, turn it into action. Don't just dream,,,Dan Gable

What is the result of imagination?
It's the cultivation of the imagination leads to the development of the ideal out of which your future will emerge.

Michael, I recall you sitting on a chair in your bedroom staring at the television watching the 1980 Grammy Awards show crying to me because you had only won 1 Grammy Award and you said, Watch La Toya, my next record I'm will sell more records and win more Grammys than anyone in the history of music... I will be the biggest and the greatest entertainer of all time. You began to write that dream all throughout your bedroom, on the walls, on the mirrors, in your books and anywhere else you could find a space. You started working much harder, creating sounds in songs that the world had never heard before, you started dancing until you literally collapse. When most artists were trying to learn how to sing and do a two-step, you were singing and moon-walking. You took your dream to a much higher level and turned it into reality, a reality of over 100 million records sold on that next album, 'Thriller.' You thereafter continued to turn every one of your dreams into reality, while inspiring the world and becoming the most recognizable, the most well-known and the most loved person in the entire world.

Words from La Toya Jackson on her brother Michael Jackson(The king of Pop)

Michael Jackson 1984 Grammy Awards

How may it be cultivated?

By exercise; it must be supplied with nourishment, or it cannot live

What is the power with which successful man build?
The mind is the very moving force with which they secure the persons and circumstances necessary to complete their plans.

What predetermines the result?
The ideal held steadily in the mind attracts the necessary condition for its fulfillment.

Vision without action is a daydream. Action without vision is a nightmare.

Here are some suggestions your vision board should cover:
Mental well being (Spirituality)
Business Goals
Living healthy
Financially stable
Personal Goals & Dreams
Relationships
Events
Trips
Hobbies

Along with your vision board. You will need a planner to help you achieve your visions. I personally use Law Of Attraction planner: Freedom Mastery Planner, which has a area for your vision board. This planner really works.

Look around less. Imagine more - Bill Proctor

IF YOU CAN IMAGINE IT, YOU CAN ACHIEVE IT; IF YOU CAN DREAM IT, YOU CAN BECOME IT.

Coaching..

The greatest leader is not necessarily the one who does the greatest things. He's the one that gets the people to do the greatest things. -Ronald Reagan

As a coach. I learned. I'm not just a coach. I'm a coach, mentor, and counselor. Each one plays a role in making the wrestler be the best he can be, on the mat and as a person in life. As shown below. You can see the different responsibilities you have when deciding to become a coach.

Coach

The Question: How?

The Focus: The present.

Aim: Improving Skills.

Objective: Raising competence.

Mentor

The Question: What?

The Focus: The future.

Aim: Developing and committing to learning goals.

Objective: Opening horizons.

Counselor

The Question: Why?

The Focus: The past.

Aim: Overcoming psychological barriers.

Objective: Building self-understanding.

When trying to achieve something in life. This is the type of person you want in your corner. You also can be behind a person being a coach, mentor, and counselor. The term 'coaching' means many different things to different people, but is generally; it's about helping individuals to solve their own problems and improve their own performance. It doesn't matter if you're a coach in wrestling, life, and business. The good coaches believe that individuals always have the answer to their own problems. They just need help to unlock them. I discovered, by helping the wrestlers learn and get better as wrestlers. I was doing the same for myself as a coach.

While teaching and showing the wrestlers the many ways to win a match. Many other ways came to me on how to do certain techniques and win matches, which I had never done before. One day in practice, a wrestler had got in a situation, a move came to me that will help him gain the advantage to score. I never saw or made the move before. I stopped the match, showed him the move that had come into my mind right at that instant. It turned out to be a great move for him. It took him all the way to become a state placer.

The move was called; drop the hip. Not only did he have great success with the move. I showed other wrestlers the move, and it helped them as well. This is just one of many moves that had come to me while coaching. This is a pure example of when you help others to be better. You will get even better. In other words. Helping others is helping yourself.

I cannot begin to tell you how many times, I've had teammates and wrestlers tell me. By wrestling with their teammate, they came up with a new move they could use themselves. All the great wrestlers know all the basic wrestling moves. But come up with a better way to do the moves that will set themselves apart from the rest. Making the move unstoppable. There's a basic wrestling move called; the single leg. The great wrestler name John Smith perfected and made it unstoppable. When a wrestler does the single leg same as John Smith. It's called the [John Smith single leg](#). Due to the way he does the move, makes it unstoppable. By him performing the move over and over., he came up with ways, to make the move unstoppable.

Remember when you are teaching or helping someone. Always look for ways that can help the person you are teaching and yourself to be the best and set you and others apart from the rest. Whenever possible always help others. You will be surprised by the more things you will learn by helping and teaching others. When you're a blessing, you will be blessed. Be happy for others, watch others be happy for you. (Not All Will Be) The right ones will.

If your coach pushes you.
If your coach disciplines you.
If your coach demands the best from you ALL the time..
Then he or she truly cares.
- McCaw Method

You want a person like this in your corner..

Role models who push us to exceed our limits, physical training that removes our spare tires, and risks that expand our sphere of comfortable action are all examples of eustress—stress that is healthful and the stimulus for growth.-*Tim Ferriss*

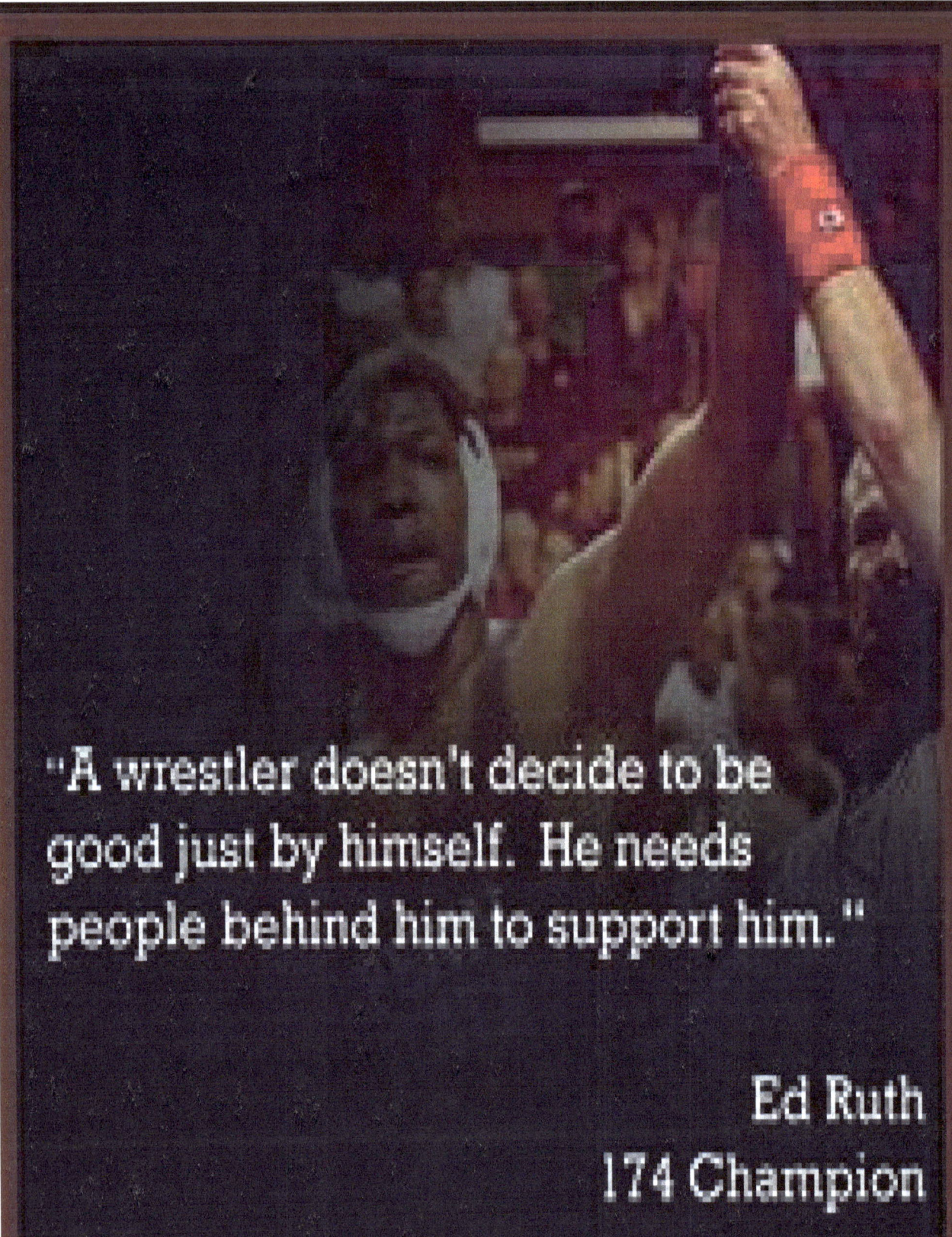

The Program.

Back in my wrestling days. There was a wrestling program here in Michigan that was super tough. From the 70's to the 80's this program was one of the top programs in the state. In the 90's the program just fell off and went way down. They were no-where near as tough as they were in the two previous decades.

A former wrestler from those glory days. Decided to take over the wrestling program, with one purpose in mind. To make the wrestling program the elite program it was back in the glory days. He put in lots of time and money and made major sacrifices for this program. I seen an interview he did. One thing stuck out to me, in that interview.

He said; other coaches do this has a hobby. For me, it's a lifestyle. He also said; he has to be an example to his wrestlers. By showing them how hard work, dedication, and vision can lead to great results. From the year 2000 to the writing of this book. That lifestyle, hard work, dedication and vision as produced. Nationally ranked teams, 6 team state championships, 5 team state runner-ups, 15 elite 8 appearances, nationally ranked individual wrestlers, 27 individual state champions, 14 individual state runner-ups, I can't count the many individual state placers & qualifiers. He can even boast about having the only 4-time undefeated division 1 state champion wrestler, who is regarded as the best high school wrestler to ever come out of Michigan.

Three of his former wrestlers are college national champions. Which one of those national champions received the Hodge Trophy. This is wrestling equivalent to the Heisman Trophy. That same wrestler was very successful at the world level.

Currently two of his former wrestler's are assistant coach's at two of the top college programs which in the country. One is the National Freestyle Developmental Coach also. He himself has received many awards has a coach. Even with his accomplishments as a coach. His greatest accomplishment is being able to get some if not all his former wrestler's college education paid for by scholarship.

My son asks me. Do I think this program will ever fall off again? I said no. This program has been built to stay one of the top teams in the state. Due to all the former wrestlers who wrestled under this coach and was a part of all those great teams. They will come back to work with the current wrestlers, to make sure they are the best they can be.

Some will become assistant coaches of the program. Who will be running practices, while the head coach can sit back and get all the glory for the team's current success from what he built and instilled in his former wrestler's? He did all the work up front. Now the program can run itself. All he has to be is a figurehead.

When you find something, you're passionate about. You will have to do what this coach did. He made major sacrifices to get the program where it is today. For you, it can be a business you want to start that helps you and others become better people. You want to set the business up, where it can run itself, and you can still reap the benefits from all your labor from the beginning. Which leads to you reaping even more benefits from others labor(Your employees). This is known as a B-business. Which is illustrated in the Robert Kiyosaki book: Rich Dad's Cashflow Quadrant.

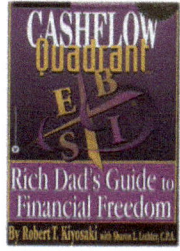

Cashflow Quadrant

48 Laws of Power #7
Get others to do the work for you, but always take the credit.

Million Dollar Question.

$1,000,000 in the bank isn't the fantasy. The fantasy is the lifestyle of complete freedom it supposedly allows.- Tim Ferriss

One day the team and I were riding on the bus, to a wrestling meet. I asked the whole team a question. I asked; What would you do if you're a senior who never made it to the state tournament in the previous three years? You advance to the match that will qualify you to wrestle in the state tournament. All you have to do is win that match.

You find out it's an opponent that you can beat with no problem; you could blow on him and pin him. He is an extremely awfully bad wrestler. The wrestler's dad approaches you. He tells you. I will give you a million dollars if you lose this match, he shows you a gym bag with the money in it. All you have to do is lose the match to get the money. What would you do?

Mostly all the wrestlers said they would take the dive. Their whole focus was on how their life would be with the money. They could buy clothes, jewelry, cars, party at the best nightclubs, date the most beautiful women and never have to worry about working.

While saying what they would do with the money. Out of nowhere one of the wrestlers said; He would tell the father; keep your money. I asked him why would you do that? He replied; You can always make money. There are many ways to make that amount of money. It will just take persistence and hard work. This is my last chance to wrestle in the state tournament.

He said something that just blew me away. He said; I don't want to be rich regretting taking the money. I will never know how I would have done at the state tournament. It would bother me deeply knowing, I put in all that work to get to that position. Then to throw it all away for something that will always be there(money).

He hit the nail on the head. In life. Most people equate success. With having money and all the luxuries, money can buy. That is very far from the truth. If that was true. **Why do rich people kill the themselves?**

If you were to ask most people what would they rather be; rich or wealthy. Most don't know the difference or would say rich. Well, there is a difference.

Rich: You have a lot of money and always focusing on getting more of it.

Wealthy: Is a person who financially stable for life, good health and take care of themselves. Surrounded by family, good friends and find the time and ways to give back to others who are less fortunate.

IMAGINE.
beining rich having all the money in world. Being able to do all the things you want to do in life. Never have to look at a price tag(Just say give me that). But have handicapped kids ,a wife and kids that hates you, family is so divided, no friends, surrounded by users cause you have money but no real friends. When your money gone they gone. Always in fear of who is trust-worthy.............Is it worth being Rich?

Which would you rather be?,,,,,,, I rather be weal-thy.

Things money can't buy:

LOVE.
As the song says by the Beatles; Can't buy me love. Money can buy lust, attraction, and power…but it can't buy love. This is because love is something intimate; something heartfelt; something mysterious. Money is none of these things. Money is simply a method of exchange – no more and no less. It's used to pay for a product or a service; its convenience, comfort, and luxury – none of which typify what human beings really need. Many of us find this lesson out the hard way. We accumulate more, only to feel emptier. This is because we are raised in a culture that glamorizes rich; which, in effect, leads to misconceptions and false beliefs.

TRUTH.
Money can buy influence, but truths are the most influential of all. Often times money is spent to push beliefs, agenda, and opinions. In the end, no matter how much money is spent on stifling or skewing the truth, it will always be revealed in the end.

TIME.
Each passing second, minute, hour, day, month and year is the time that you will never get back; you're one minute closer to dying. This is depressing but truthful. Our life starts to fade away from the moment we are born. The rich have spent lots of money to extend their lives only to find out that they die around the same age as everyone else. No amount of money will be able to turn back time. Take life, moment-by-moment, while experiencing it to the fullest.

PEACE.
Your thoughts are the only thing that will bring you peace. One aspect of this is accepting when bad things happen and turning it into a positive experience. Your peace shouldn't depend on your bank statement. It's how you train your mind, set expectations, and define what peace really means to you.

Talents.
The gifts and abilities that you possess in your mind and body are priceless. While money can certainly help develop a talent, it will never be able to purchase a talent or skill. We have the ability to learn a skill or talent; this will never be able to be bought with money. The mental processes and dexterity of the mind and body will never be purchasable…they 're invaluable.

Health.
Money can buy healthcare and medicine; it cannot replace natural health once it's gone. At the same time, activities like exercise, preventative medicine, and natural self-care cost little to nothing. Celebrities will spend a lot of money to keep their natural beauty. Aging is; wrinkling and gray hair. Surgical procedures that implant plastic and other medicinal substances into the body? This is not at all natural.

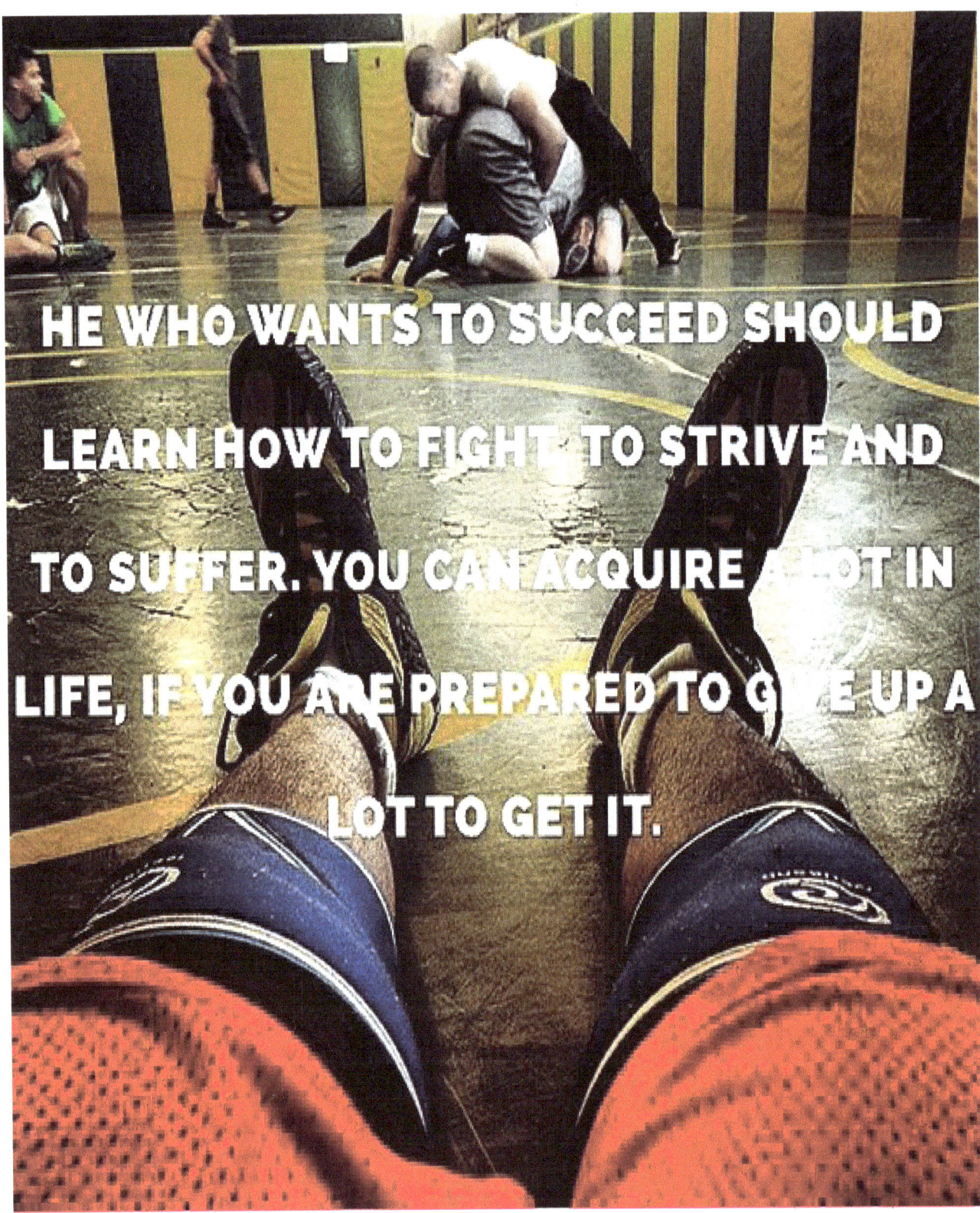

Manners.
Rude people exist everywhere. How to treat someone respectfully does not come from money. There are more rich and entitled snobs than there are those of modest means. The money will put you into a higher class, but it certainly does not make you have manners.

True Friends.
Money attracts people who want to be your friend; it doesn't guarantee true friendship. True friends love one another. True friends are the ones there during the good times and still there during the bad times. Money and possessions don't matter to a true friend...you matter.

KNOWLEDGE.
The information that you accumulate, the elements of your intellect, and the ways that you exhibit wisdom can never be bought. Have you ever wondered why some of the richest people seem to be a little off or crazy insane? This is because money or something else has influenced their thought processes. Many rich people have stated how money makes them feel 'invincible,' and as a result, have made some bad choices. So it's not only the acquisition of this knowledge that makes it invaluable, it's how you apply this knowledge...neither of which money can buy.

As you can see, having money doesn't make you successful. Money is something people have. Some have a lot, and some have very little. It's up to you how you measure your success. Never let someone else perspective, determine if you are successful or not.

"If" a wrestler can walk off the mat after practice or a match being able to say; I gave everything I had today. Then he's successful.
"If" a person is able to overcome the enormous obstacles that face them, after being released from prison and become an asset to society. That person is successful.
"If" people can leave from your presence feeling better about themselves. That person is successful.
"If" a person can overcome drug and alcohol addiction. That person is successful.
"If" you have family and friends that love, care and want the best for you. Then you're successful.
"If" you're providing for your family. You're successful.

I can go on and on. Just know; success is not based on money and material possessions. Success is based on your definition of a fulfilled life which many leave this earth without living one.

Success by definition:
The *favorable or prosperous termination of attempts or endeavors; the accomplishment of one's goals.*

Remember. Everybody do not have the same definition of success. Only you can determined that.

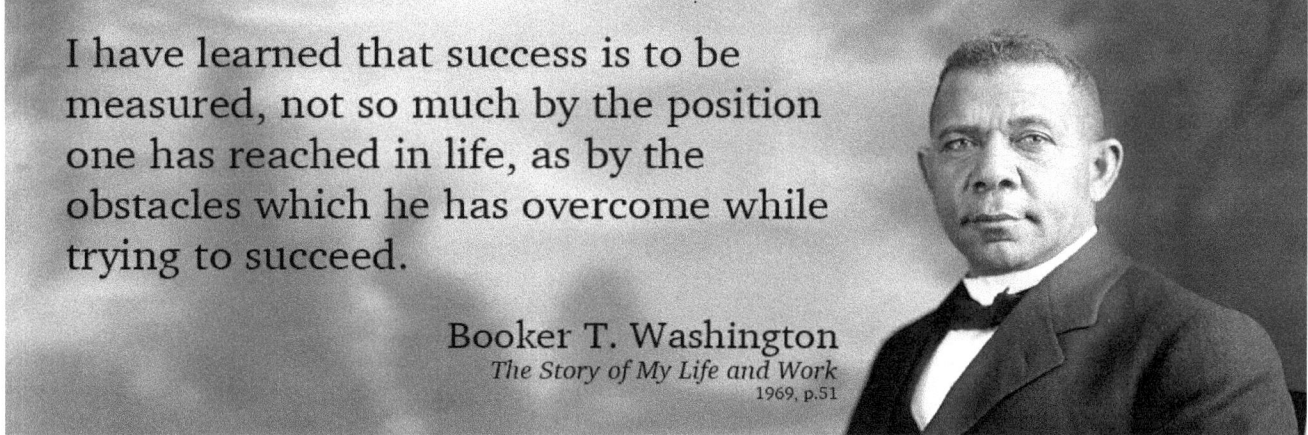

Just because you're struggling does not mean you're failing........

If you want to increase your success rate, double your failure rate - *Thomas J. Watson*

When you double your self-worth, you can double your net worth. You can never exceed the height of your self-image.

The sweetest revenge of all is success. Nothing makes people crazier than someone living a GOOD LIFE....
Let no one control your destiny! The pen that writes your life story must be held in your own hand.....

The 10 by 10 rule to a million dollars:

ONE'S BEST SUCCESS COMES AFTER THEIR GREATEST DISAPPOINTMENTS.

Remember: "Success is not measured by what you accomplish, but by the opposition you have encountered, and the courage with which you have maintained the struggle against overwhelming odds.

It's not where you're at or where you're going it's where you've been and how you got here.

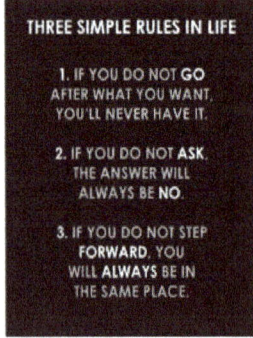

THREE SIMPLE RULES IN LIFE

1. IF YOU DO NOT **GO** AFTER WHAT YOU WANT, YOU'LL NEVER HAVE IT.

2. IF YOU DO NOT **ASK**, THE ANSWER WILL ALWAYS BE **NO**.

3. IF YOU DO NOT STEP **FORWARD**, YOU WILL **ALWAYS** BE IN THE SAME PLACE.

Success is not final, failure is not fatal: it is the courage to continue that counts.

-Winston Churchill

THE BOTTOM LINE

SUCCESSFUL PEOPLE CONSISTENTLY DO WHAT NORMAL PEOPLE REFUSE TO DO

Work hard in silence, let your success be your noise.

The Haunting

Wrestling is one sport that will haunt you to no end. If you know, you didn't give it your all, or achieve what you know you could have achieved, if you would have put forth a little extra effort, what if you did something stupid, like not making weight at the state qualifying tournament.

This will bother you for the rest of your days. I can't begin to tell all the stories of people I know that didn't achieve what they know they could have achieved in wrestling. The things they would do to try to make themselves feel better about themselves for not achieving in wrestling. Right now as I'm writing this book. I'm dealing with a person who I don't know what school he wrestled for if he placed in the state or even wrestled in college. What I do know is; He became the A.D. for the school I wrestled for then coached. When he became A.D. after the other A.D. retirement.

He had done so many things that weren't right, which hurt a lot of people. He tried ending a returning state placer senior season. He has lied, been 2 faced and outright evil. Now that he's retired and gotten older. He gets drunk and texts me how he regrets all the dirty things he said and did to me and others involved with the wrestling program. He gets so drunk till he verbally attacks coaches that have coached me and coached with me.

He tries to take credit for former wrestler's that myself and my coaching partners have coached and had very successful careers. He has gone so far, till he has tried to trick me into posting on our social media page saying; I'm the reason for the bad things that happen to the wrestling program at my school and not him. He has called me every name in the book but just short of the n-word. Well now he is just out right calling me the N-word..

Treating to kick my a** in which he didn't realize I wasn't far from him, so he escapes from getting hurt. I've even blocked him on my phone. He gets a new number to start his mess. What it all comes down to. He is in the 3rd period of his life. He's looking back on all the things he has done to others, and it's tarring him up inside.

Now, mind you, the things he had done when I was involved with the program, happened over 15 years ago. I and everyone involved have moved on and want nothing to do with him. He knows this, which causes him to drink to medicate the pain he has brought on himself. This is no way to live, especially at his age now. I have to look back and seen how I hurt others and caused pain.

There is no way around it. I to will have to reap the things I've done to others. I know this. In which wrestling and my higher power will help me face them head-on. All drugs and alcohol will just make it worst in the long run. All I can do now is treat people right at this point in my life while facing and reaping the things I've done, and mistakes have I've made in the past.

The best way to apologize to the people. Is a changed life and behavior. We all know that old saying. Actions speak louder than words.

Reflection of You

Show respect even to people who don't deserve it; not as a reflection of their character, but as a reflection of yours.- Dave Willis

When people saw me wrestle and seen some of the move's I did on the mat. They would ask others around them, where did he learn that at. They replied he must have learned that from his coach. As a matter of fact, I saw his coach do the same move back in the day when he wrestled. They would go on to say. Most wrestlers are reflections of their coach. That is so true. As a wrestler and coach. I saw many wrestlers who wrestled just like their coach. Somewhere good, some were bad, and some were very bad. I knew they wrestled like their coach because I either wrestled with, against, saw them wrestle at a meet or tournament when their coaches where wrestlers.

I coached many wrestlers who wrestled a lot like myself. There was one who wrestled just like me. It got to the point, where I hated practicing with him because I was wrestling myself. I had to figure out ways to beat myself. One of the things I use to do to him. I would talk trash to him, telling him he can't score on me or get a certain move on me. That worked most of the time because I knew he had self-doubt about himself when it came to him wrestling me. Plus I am the one who taught him everything he knew about wrestling, so he believed me. He didn't know I was more afraid of him than he was of me. I knew the words I spoke had value to him because I'm his coach. That gave me influence over him.

When his high school wrestling career was over. In which he was a 3-time state qualifier. In his senior year, he went to the state tournament 49-0. After winning his first match at state, he was injured and couldn't compete in the rest of the tournament. I told him what I would do when I had to wrestle him in practice. He said dang, it worked. You had me believing I couldn't do a lot of the things I wanted to do when I wrestled you. Since you were the coached I just believed you. You don't have to be a coach to influence a person.

A parent is a child's first teacher. Children are like a sponge; they absorb all the information presented to them. Usually, the first ones presenting that information is the parent(s). 99% of the time when you see hatred towards another race or religion, it was taught as a child by their parents. Now the kids or a reflection of their parents. Which is another example of a generational curse?

I've asked people why do they believe in certain religious beliefs and political parties. They really couldn't tell me why. Most all said the same thing. It was how they were raised to believe. Never learning for themselves why they believe the way they do. When you have influence or power over an individual or group. Be sure to carry yourself in a way that makes people want to emulate or be a total reflection of you. Be a person who doesn't see race or religion, but see everyone as a human being. Be a person of your word. Never speak negativity of others. Always wish the best for everyone. Be a person who go get what he wants and willing to put a great amount of effort to get it. Be loyal, faithful and trust-worthy.

Remember in the advice section of this book. I said look at the person giving you advice or telling you something to do. If that person hasn't had success at what you are trying to achieve, don't listen to them. You can have the same mind as the person I just described. This will make you even more successful in life, and make people want to be like you or in other words be a reflection of you.

NOTE:
If you **LOVE** yourself, you love others. If you **HATE** yourself, you hate others. Relationships with others, are only **YOU** mirrored.

FACT: Haters don't really hate you. They hate themselves because you're a reflection of what they wish to be.
People who are not happy with themselves cannot possibly be happy for you...

When you want it MORE.

My first year as a coach. I had these plans on how I am going to make these kids very good wrestlers. I was going to show them winning wrestling moves, how to get in top condition, how to push themselves to be the best, stay after practice, show moves they can work on at home, get wrestling books to study, figure out ways for them to go to wrestling camps and wrestle over the summer. Then reality hit me. On the first day of practice. I think maybe 7 or 8 kids showed up for practice. The ones that did show barely wanted to do anything or pay attention. As days went on, other kids would join the team but would miss practice or show up late. I never could get the whole team together in any given practice. I was always re-showing moves for kids who miss the previous practice.

When it was time to wrestle in the matches and tournaments. Some kids wouldn't show up or wrestle the way I knew they could wrestle. This was very frustrating to me. Most of that season I stayed mad at the kids, for not wanting it as much as I did. I remember this particular match a kid loss. I was telling him what he did wrong and what we could do to make him better and win the next time. I could see in his face; he really wasn't paying any attention to me. It didn't upset him at all for losing the match. I told the other coach, how the kid reacted to losing the match.

He seen how upset I was from the kids' reaction. He asked me why am I upset? I told him. The kid act like it was nothing. I said to him wouldn't you be upset also? He said something to me that made me even madder. He said; **NO!!!**. He said as long as you are doing your part in helping them to get better, and they are not willing to put in the effort or listen to the people that can help them. That's on them, not you. He also said the old saying. You can lead a horse to water, but it's up to the horse to drink. I went home that evening, thought about what he said.

I realized, he was right. If they don't want to do what it takes to get better or make the sacrifices. It's on them. I also realize some of these kids were causing me to forget certain techniques, due to the fact of having to repeat the same techniques over and over due to kids missing practice.

The next day in practice. I told the kids if you don't want to do what it takes to be a good wrestler. It's on them. I will help the ones who really want to be good. I let them know; if they lose a match. I won't lose my car, my house or anything would happen to my family or me. I informed them. I was there to help them achieve, not only in wrestling but also in life. You don't want that. Don't waste my time or your time. From that day on. I was basically stress-free. I also turned out some pretty good wrestlers.

You would think. I would have learned from that experience. Just recently. I tried to help a co-worker who was wanting to find another job. But didn't have a computer. I informed her, I had a computer that I could sell to her dirt cheap. She said okay call me to set up a day to see it. I called her she wouldn't answer the phone. I saw her at work; she would tell me to call again, then she would act like I was pestering her to buy the computer. She started avoiding me. I said to myself forget it. I was trying to help her, she doesn't want my help, and now it's making me look bad.

In your life span you will come across people, loved ones and someone you're in a relationship with, who will say; I need and want your help, but when you try to help them, their actions show they really don't want your help at all. Those are the people you need to stay away from. They can cause you to be brought down in the process. When a person is drowning you throw them a life preserver.

When you're trying to pull them up from drowning. You can be pulled down also and cause you to drown. In most situations, it is best to help from afar or not at all. That way you don't get brought down to that person's level. You have to love people from a distance and the space and time to get their mind right before you let them back into your life.

One part of loving people: You have to give things up. Sometimes you even have to give them up.

Be careful who you feel sorry 😏 for. Some people are good at lying & playing victim 👀🤔🫰🙏✊💪🙌

Why not YOU?

On day while coaching at a qualifying tournament for the state tournament. A senior wrestler from a less prominent city. He wrestle a kid, who is a senior also from one of the wealthy cities here in Michigan. Not only was the wrestler's family well off. He's a good wrestler.

My wrestler totally dominated him. All of a sudden in the middle of the 3rd period, he started crying, he let the other wrestler comeback in points then pin him. He basically gave-up the match, which led to his opponent advancing to the state tournament. I ask him why did you just give up the match like that? He said; coach look at me and look at him.

I said, yea what am I looking at. He said; that kid is very well off living in a nice neighborhood. I'm living in a not so well off neighborhood. I live with my aunt and not mother. I don't even know who my father is. I said; what's that got to do with you giving up like that? He said; I told you why. His life is better than mine. So I wasn't supposed to be winning the match.

I was just floored by what he said. I told him his thinking is all messed-up. I explain to him. His parents made that life for him. He had nothing to do with it at all. He still has to grow up and make a life for himself. I also told him you and him will have the same opportunities while growing up. Yes, he may have a slight advantage, because of his parents. With a don't quit attitude. You can make a great life for you and your children.

I told him never put himself beneath anyone, never think you can't have the best in life, because of your surroundings or income level. By him giving-up in that match. He created a regret that he will have to live with for the rest of his life. The main reason this kid had thinking like this. Is due to what has been put in his head as a child by his family members. In which I explained earlier. It's called a **generational curse**.

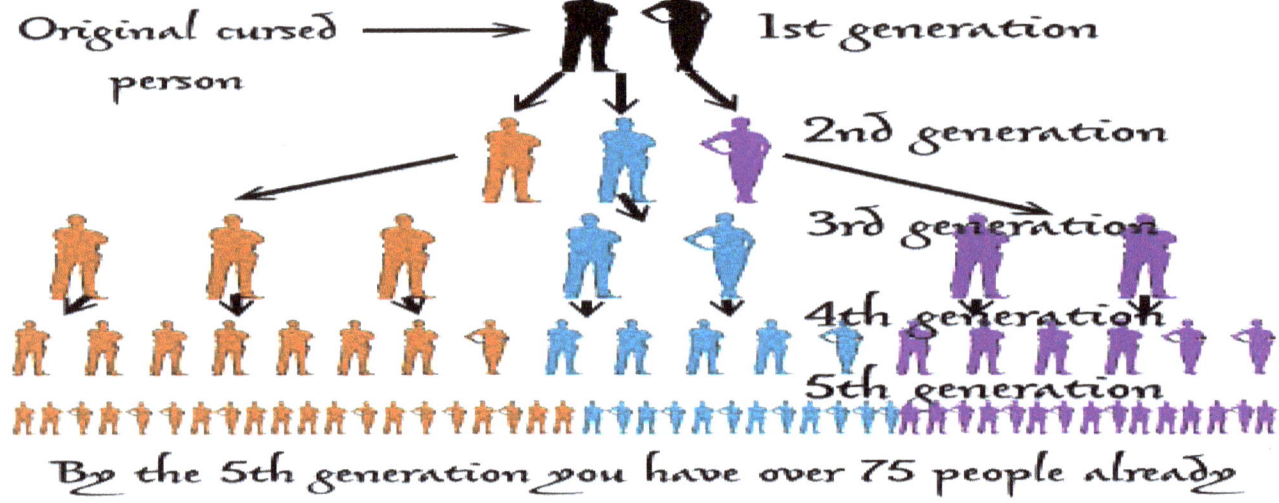

It was put in his head how to view people who have money and living a better life than you. They're viewed as better than you and get all the breaks in life. You're told you can never be like them, so don't try to be. This is something myself and many others have been told for many years. So much so till we believe we're less than everyone we meet and can never be an asset to society. I still to this day struggle with believing in myself. My biggest obstacle is my mind, but I'm gaining control over it. This 3rd book is a pure example of me gaining control over my mind and believing in myself.

I've said earlier. You are what you say you are. You also deserve the best that life has to offer. Never believe you don't deserve the best in life, WHY NOT!!!!!!! You eat, sleep, breath and bleed just like everyone else. The secret to being successful is **STRUGGLE.** Nobody wants to struggle to get the best that life has to offer. To struggle will cause you to gain knowledge and wisdom. When you do get to the point in life where you want to be. Then lose it. You know how to get it back and still live your dream life.

When everything is giving to a person, then he loses it. He doesn't know how to get it back, because he was never taught or had to struggle to get all the best life has to offer. In cases when that happens. People have been known to go crazy or even kill themselves.

Remember you can have the best just like everybody else. Never think you're not worthy of having the best that life has to offer. **Why not YOU**!!!!!!!!

why not you?

Why Not YOU!!!!!!!!!!!!

15 Bed Time Affirmations

1. I am calm and peaceful
2. I've done my best today
3. I'm grateful for this day's opportunities
4. My mind is restful
5. I'm proud of myself
6. Everything I did today leads to a better tomorrow
7. My heart is grateful
8. My heart is pure
9. My body is relaxed
10. I'm happy with my accomplishments
11. I'm proud of my efforts
12. I'm safe
13. I'm filled with content
14. Tomorrow is a new day full of possibilities
15. I rejoice in what I've learned today

Knowing your OPPONENT'S

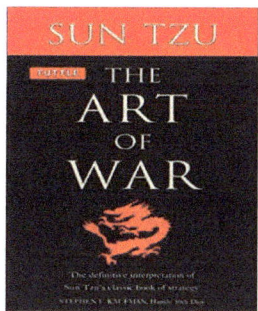

The best way to win in a wrestling match is to know your opponent. Knowing what your opponent what moves setups, what he can and cannot stop, can he go a full match without getting tired, does he delay matches when he's tired. There are many other things you can find out about your opponent by just watching him wrestle in a match.

Your toughest opponent is the one who knows everything about you. This person is your teammate. This is someone who you practice with every day, did everything you did to be the best. Even though you're better than him, it is very hard for you to beat him, because he knows so much about you and the things you do on the mat. In most cases this person is in the same weight class as you, both of you have to wrestle off to see who will wrestle varsity for the team.

This can get very ugly. I've seen wrestlers who lost the wrestle-off get mad, say mean things, throw punches and not want to talk to the person who they lost the wrestle-off to. Most of the time if a wrestler keeps losing the wrestle-off; he goes to another weight class where he can be in the starting lineup. Then he's able to accept losing the wrestle-off and just move on from there.

In life; when you set out to achieve the things you want in life or want better for your life. There's going to be people who say you can't do a certain thing. Those people are your opponents, in other words, it is expected you will have negative people say things to you and about you, this is something you already know about people period.

Your toughest opponent will be loved ones, close friends and even your spouse's. They're the ones who usually come at you the hardest; It will be hard for you to overlook the things they say because they're so close to you.

Due to the things you want to achieve, you may not want to associate with them anymore because all they will do is bring you negativity and bring you down. Once they realize you don't want to associate with them anymore.

They will verbally attack you, say mean things behind your back and not ever want to talk to you. Eventually, they just give up and move on.

You can love someone and still cut them out your life..

Know your OPPONENT!!!

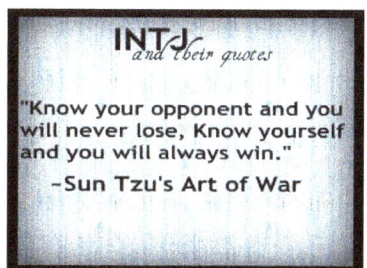

The Art of War is a must read for all areas of your **LIFE**.....

Team-mates/Friends
Not every friend that looks like a friend is a friend.

While competing at the state tournament. I advanced to the semi-final round, if I win this match I'll be in the state finals, it was a close match in which I came out ahead and advanced to the state finals. After that match, I received a lot of congratulations from teammates, friends, and people I didn't even know. But there was one congratulation that stood out among all of them.

This congratulation was from my teammate who also was in the semi-finals but had lost his match. He said; congratulations on 2nd in the state. It didn't hit me till a few minutes later. Now mind you I had not wrestled in the finals yet, but he just knew I was going to loose.

I thought to myself; what a thing to say. This particular teammate's father helped me to get where I was at in wrestling by taking me to all the Sunday tournaments, getting me in different camps and working out with me. My teammate himself thought he was God's gift to wrestling. For him to say what he said showed me right then, he wasn't there for me and that he didn't like I did something better than him.

This was somebody I considered a teammate and a friend. Come to find out he was neither. He was just somebody I was on the wrestling team with. It didn't stop there, he did and said things that a teammate or friend wouldn't do or say. To this day he lets it be known that he is better than me. There are other teammates who I thought were much closer than just teammates. I was wrong. Life has a way of showing you that things are not always what they appear to be. Life has taught me to watch who you call your friend.

The very one you call a friend, may be the very one plotting against you or hope you fail. I read a quote that said; **if you don't want your enemies to know your business don't tell your friend.** The best way to find out who your real friends are, look to see who's there when you are at a low point in your life or need help.

Everybody is your friend when things are going well for you or when you are doing for them. At this point in my life, I can honestly say I may have one or two people I can call friends. The lyric's to the Whodini song; <u>Friends</u> says it all.

<u>Don't surround yourself with people that don't wish you well. You can't kill them but can take them out of your circle.</u>

Do What's Right.

I coached a wrestler who was extremely good. In his senior year in High School he went undefeated. He is by far one of the best wrestlers I've ever coached. In the wrestling world, he had what is known as a great shot. It was totally unstoppable. But in the majority of his match's he did his shots wrong. Which would cause a lot of presure to be put on his shoulders. Even with that presure being placed on his shoulders, he was still able to score, what is known as a takedown. I told him you can't keep doing the shot that way. It's gonna catch up to you and cause you to lose a match or not be able to wrestle.

Well he was able to do that all the way to the reginal finals tournament, in which you have to place in the top four in order to quilify for the state tournament. He won a tough finals match, which came down to him needing to score a takedown. He did that wrong shot but was still able to score the takedown to win the match.

After the match he complained how bad his shoulders was hurting. There is a two week break between reginals and the state tournament. So he seen a doctor during the break. It turns out he did a whole lot of damage to his shoulders by shooting the wrong way. His shoulders were damage so bad , he couldn't even wrestle in the state tournament. Due to so much pain. He was forced to drop out of the state tournament. Which killed any chances of him being a undefeated, State Champion wrestler.

This is something he has to live with for the rest of his life. If only he did what he was suppose to do. He would be living a happy life, as a state champion wrestler. But instead he has to live with the pain of not doing the move the right, which cost him something only few can dream of;STATE CHAMPION. Also by him not doing what he was suppose to do. It killed any chances of me coaching a state chmpion wrestler. All my time and money became a total waste. Even though I coached many good wrestlers after him. I just never had the fire in me to make a serious effort on getting a wrestler to becoming a state champion wrestler.

I to had something simular happen to me. Accept it wasn't on a wrestling mat, it was in my marriage. I kept doing something, I knew she wouldn't approve of. Not only she wouldn't aprove of it. I myself wouldn't approve if she did the same thing. I kept doing it over and over, till it caught up with me.

My wife seen what I was doing and for how long I was doing it. She became enrage, which made her want to divorce me and want nothing to do with me. In which I don't blame her. I could have prevented this by just doing the right thing. Now I have to live with this for the rest of my life. Now this wonderful lady who really cared for me and put me first in everything she did. Now all her time and love for me, has become a total waste for her. This did cause her to be hurt, have trust issuses and never want to be involved with a man ever again.

When you know to do **RIGHT,** Do it. In most situations, not only do you have to live with the choices you make. The choices you make can affect others, either in a positive way or in a negative way. I'm sure my wrestler wish he could turn back time and do his whole senior wrestling season over. I wish I could do it over. I would be more considerate of my wifes feelings. [Sorry don't heal wounds.](#)

In wrestling the best counter to any move, is not get caught in your oppenents move. In life the best way to heal a wound, is not cause the wound. My wife didn't deserve the pain I caused her. Her leaving me is the best thing for her life. Now she can live a happy fulfilled life. All can say is: **I LOVE YOU!!!!**

Thanks for all the wonderful memories and the love you bestowed on me. I will never **ever ever ever ever** forget you and never stop **Loving you.**

You Always know it's the right thing, when in the end there's peace..

Oprah Winfrey

Overtime

Criticism is something we can avoid easily. By saying nothing, doing nothing, and being nothing.

Aristotle

Legacy......

A legacy is something that is left behind after a person has moved on or passed. Legacy is more about sharing what you have learned, not just what you have earned, and bequeathing values over valuables, as material wealth is only a small fraction of your legacy. A more holistic definition of legacy is when you are genuinely grounded in offering yourself and making a meaningful, lasting and energizing contribution to humanity by serving a cause greater than your own.

A legacy requires that you embrace your uniqueness, passionately immersing your whole self into life so that your gift will be to all and that you take responsibility to ensure that it will have a life beyond that of you, its creator, outliving and outlasting your time on earth.

Legacy germinates unity consciousness, is not an entity but an ongoing activity and is what you do between here and eternity. The lens of legacy gives you a view of your life from a generational perspective, where you become aware of the desire to live beyond yourself, focused on making a difference in the lives of others and giving back.

The legacy you leave is the life you lead, and therefore legacy is the residue of a life well lived. Your life matters as everything that you say and do is a deposit into your legacy. Creating your legacy is a pathway resulting in a deep sense of significance; where true meaning is found somewhere beyond the pursuit of success, which results in a ripple effect that positively impacts society. Inherently, when you shift to living your legacy, your influence comes from who you are authentically at the core, and you measure value and life purpose other than by emphasis on accomplishments, wealth, recognition, prestige, acclaim, power or position.

The head wrestling coach, I had my first year in high school. Was a well-known in the wrestling arena. He is a wrestling Hall of Fame in the state of Pennsylvania, along with being in the Hall of Fame for the University of Michigan. The great Cliff Keen was his coach. Yes, the name you see on all the wrestling equipment today.

He coached a nationally ranked teams, nationally ranked wrestlers and many state placers. He coached the only state championship team.

Members of the varsity wrestling team are: FIRST ROW: Rick Pittman, Larry Michalik, Mark Ellis, Gary Pate, Paul Goosby, Kevin Tracy. SECOND ROW: Ed Willis, Rick Hislop, Mark Fox, Kevin Rize, Bob Lusk, Bob Colaianne

When he passed. I couldn't wait to hear all the war stories from his past wrestlers. I really wanted to know what it was like being a part of those great teams from the past. Just think to be on those teams striking fear in everyone, when they step into the gym.

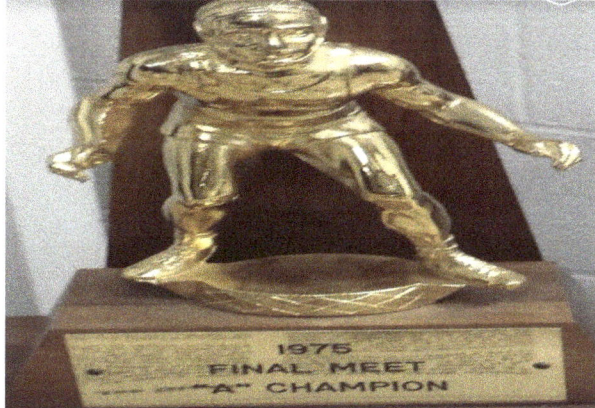

I did get to meet a lot of the great wrestlers from the past, who wrestled on all those great teams. I ask every one of them what was it like wrestling on those great teams and being feared as a wrestler. I received the same response from every last one of them. They just said; it was fun. Really didn't say much after that.

What they really wanted to talk about. Was how this man touched their lives in a way no one has ever done. They had long conversations, on how he taught them values that they use to this day, how to grow up to be a real man, how he believed in them when no-one else did. Taught them how to treat people, how he spent time with them, going on camping trips, not seeing them as a piece of meat. The memories they told last the two days of the viewing and into the funeral. None of it was about wrestling. Seeing and hearing all this. Made me think and BOOM!!!!! Everything came back to me, like a whirlwind.

My first year wrestling in high school was his last year in coaching. I started remembering all the great things he taught me when it came to wrestling. What really stood out for me. Is what he did for me off the mat. Like I said before. When I got to high school. I had to start all over. So I wasn't the top guy on the team. I took some lumps in matches and in practice. I was raised in the church. I never heard somebody say; Jesus Christ, so much until I started wrestling in high school. It would be more like GEEEEEEEEEEEEEEEEEEEEEEEEESUS CHRIST!!!!!!!!!!!!!!!!!!!! or **YOUR SELLING THE FARM!!!!!!!!!** When I heard that. I knew I was messing up. Needless to say, I heard that a lot. He was a teacher in the school. I made sure to never walk past his classroom. I just knew he was going to call me into his classroom, to tell me all the things I did wrong, and what I needed to work on to be a better wrestler.

I pretty much knew what I needed to work on. It was **EVERYTHING!!!**. I already had low self-esteem. Didn't need him to add to it. Well, sure enough, I had to walk past his classroom. Guess what? Like I said. He called me into his classroom. He called me by a name I hate(Timmy). Walking into his classroom I was thinking here we go. He's going to tell me all the bad things I do on the mat, what I need to work on and how I can get better.

I get into the room, prepared for what's about to happen next. He told me to have a seat. I'm thinking here we go. What happened next was something I wasn't prepared for. He asked me how I was doing, how was school, how was life treating me, what are my likes and dislikes.

We ended up talking about everything except wrestling. I was in total **shock**. Here's a man who actually cared about me. He made me feel like I was somebody. This was huge. As a child growing up into my teen years. I was always told what a failure I am. I had a step dad who made it known that I was nothing, and he treated me like nothing. My coach made me realize. Even though I'm not the best wrestler on the team. I'm still **somebody**.

It's not all about sports. It's about treating people right no matter their background or skill level. Pretty much every day after that. I would go to his classroom to sit and talk to him, even after the season had ended. In those talks, I learned a lot about life. When we did talk about wrestling. He always said. He has a picture frame ready for me to put my wrestling photo in. Which will be placed in the wrestling Hall of Fame at the school. Even though he wasn't coaching anymore. He still took the time to see how I'm doing and even came to see me wrestle. There is a lot more this man did for myself and his former wrestlers. I'll be writing for days. I will say; He gave us something he would never get back. It was his; **TIME...** When a person gives you their time. That says you are **important.**

Nobody likes to waste their time. Not only did he leave a big impression on myself and other wrestlers. He left a bigger impression on the school.

My school mascot is the zebras. He named wrestling team, the Wolfpack. He said you don't want to be a zebra. A zebra is an animal of prey. A wolf hunts and destroys animals of prey.

The wrestling team has had the Wolfpack name for over 40 years. School administration has tried to get away from the Wolfpack name. It won't go away. So they just left it as the Wolfpack. One day while listening to a local radio station.

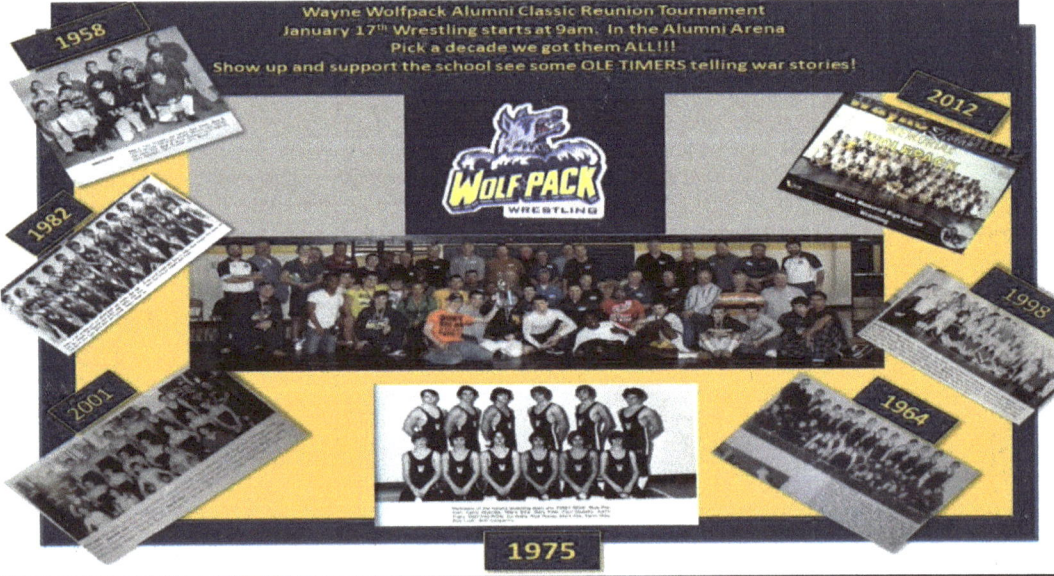

They were talking about High School mascots names. A listener called in, to asked, why is there a school with two mascot's name? He said the school itself is the zebra's but the wrestling team is the Wolfpack. The radio personality couldn't answer the question. I was like WOW!!!! That's awesome.

Even when I went to my class reunion. My classmates were bragging about being zebras. They looked at me and said we know you're not a zebra, you're a Wolfpack. I said. That's right and don't forget it.

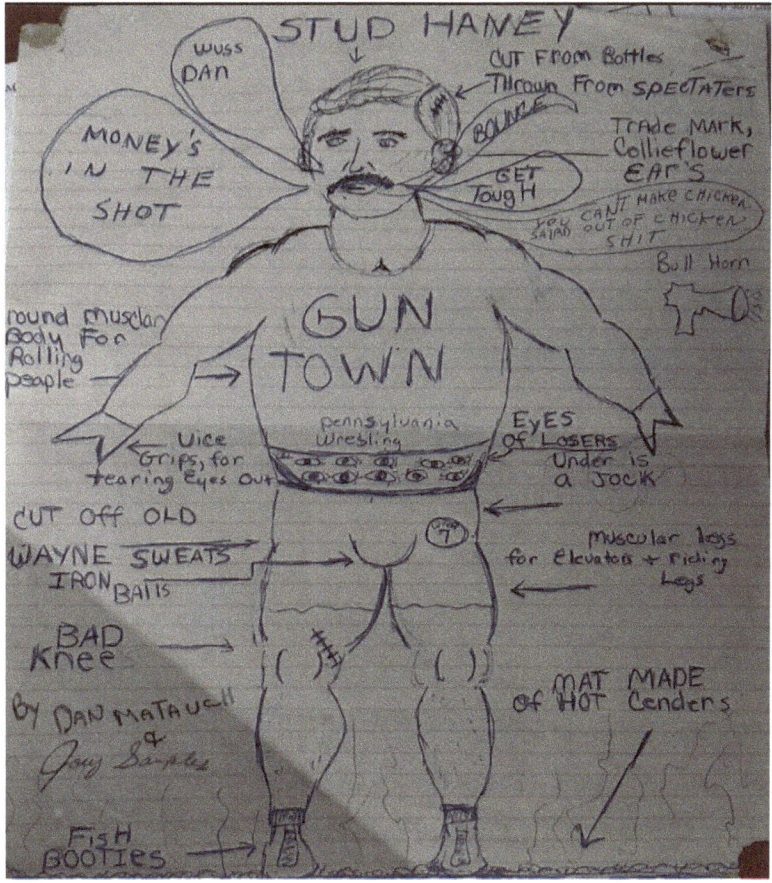

This picture was drawn by two of his former wrestler's while he was coaching them. This shows the affect, love and admiration they had for him. Oh yes he was a tough old dude.

Two other former wrestlers of his and I have gone on to coach other schools. Each school had great success unlike ever before in their history. It was due to the teaching and coaching gave to us by our coach. One school had a coaching retirement party.

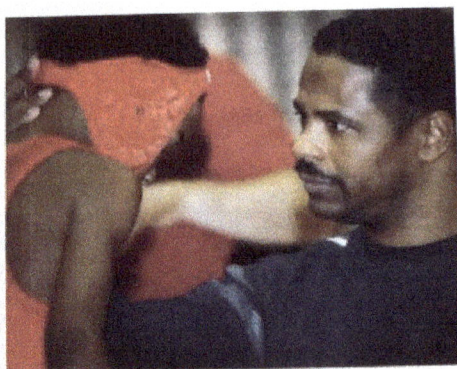

All the parents and wrestlers had nothing but praise for him. I even spoke. Everything that was said was so similar to the things that were said at our coach funeral. Our coach has been gone for almost 20 years now. But as you can see. His memory and legacy still lives on. Which makes me think of the old saying: You will never see a U-Haul behind a hearse. In other words. You can't take anything with you. So what are you going to leave behind?

Something to think about:

Many famous people have died. Such as Singers, actors, dancers, authors, athletes, rappers, etc. If you were ask when where they born or died. Most of us wouldn't know either. What is known is how great they were at their craft. Their graves have their date of birth and date of death.

Now think what's between those two dates? It's a DASH, separating those two dates. It's a small but actually a big symbol of that person's life. We are all living in our DASH right now.

We know our date of birth but don't know when we're going to depart this life. You too can have an effect on peoples life's, by becoming someone who inspires, motivate and help others. Just know how you live your life(Your DASH)now, will determine your legacy. Or how you will be remembered. Make the best of this life(DASH)you've been given and you too can leave something of meaning, that will live long after you have left this life.

Your DASH

You can learn ways to live your DASH. In my book called The DASH...

Conclusion

In the END...

When you become old and can't wrestle anymore. This sport will have sped up the aging process, making you look older than you really are. Cause major arthritis. Some have cauliflower ear so bad till they look like Yoda from Star Wars. If you were going to be grumpy and old, wrestling would make you even more grumpy. I've seen interviews with some older wrestlers. Who are all crippled up and in pain? Mostly, due to wrestling for a very long period of time.

Their body is pretty much out of whack. The old wrestlers themselves would tell you wrestling has really had a toll on their body. They were asked; if you knew you were going to end up like this from wrestling. Would you have wrestled or do it all over again? They all replied, saying HELL YEA!!!!!!!!!!!!! It was worth every bit of it. All the hard work, all the dedication, all the struggles, all the failures, all which led to great rewards on and off the mat.

A famous saying in wrestling is; wrestling is hard, life is easy because I wrestled. You don't have to be a wrestler to feel the same way. We all will become old, and not be able to do the things we used to do when we were young. That's just a fact of life. Wouldn't you want to look back on your life? To see all the hard work you put in, the struggles you went through, the fears you overcame, the doubts you had. Then be able to say; I am a **<u>CHAMPION..</u>**

You too can raise your hands like a wrestler, and say I am a CHAMPION!!!!!!!!!!!!!

Your life must mean something. Otherwise, your living was in vain.

Bonus Chapter

Perseverance

noun: perseverance

Persistence in doing something despite difficulty or delay in achieving success.

1. Tenacity
2. Determined
3. Staying Power
4. Diligent
5. Dedication
6. Commitment
7. Endurance
8. Stamina

In the many years I've been around wrestling. I've been bless to see many great things in wrestling. But I must say some things just don't make sense. While as a coach. I had 2 kids who were seniors and 1 was a junior, in which the 2 seniors became All-State wrestlers. The junior qualified for the state tournament.

The one kid. I became his coach in his senior year. He had wrestled in junior high school and attended many wrestling camps. So one would think he's going to be one of the most skilled wrestlers on the team. Well, that wasn't the case. I couldn't believe what I was seeing. With all that experience, he was not one of the best on the team. He wasn't very athletic at all.

The one thing he had going for him. He was a very hard worker and never gave up. Even with that, he would lose matches he should have won. The matches he did win would go into unnecessary over-time. I would always tell him you're not going to make it to the state tournament wrestling the way he has.

In the post season tournaments. It didn't look good for him at all. In Michigan, in order to qualify for the state tournament. A wrestler as to place in the top 4 in district's then top 4 in regional's to wrestle in the state tournament. The district tournament is the only tournament where the wrestler gets seated, regional and state tournament is by a formula.

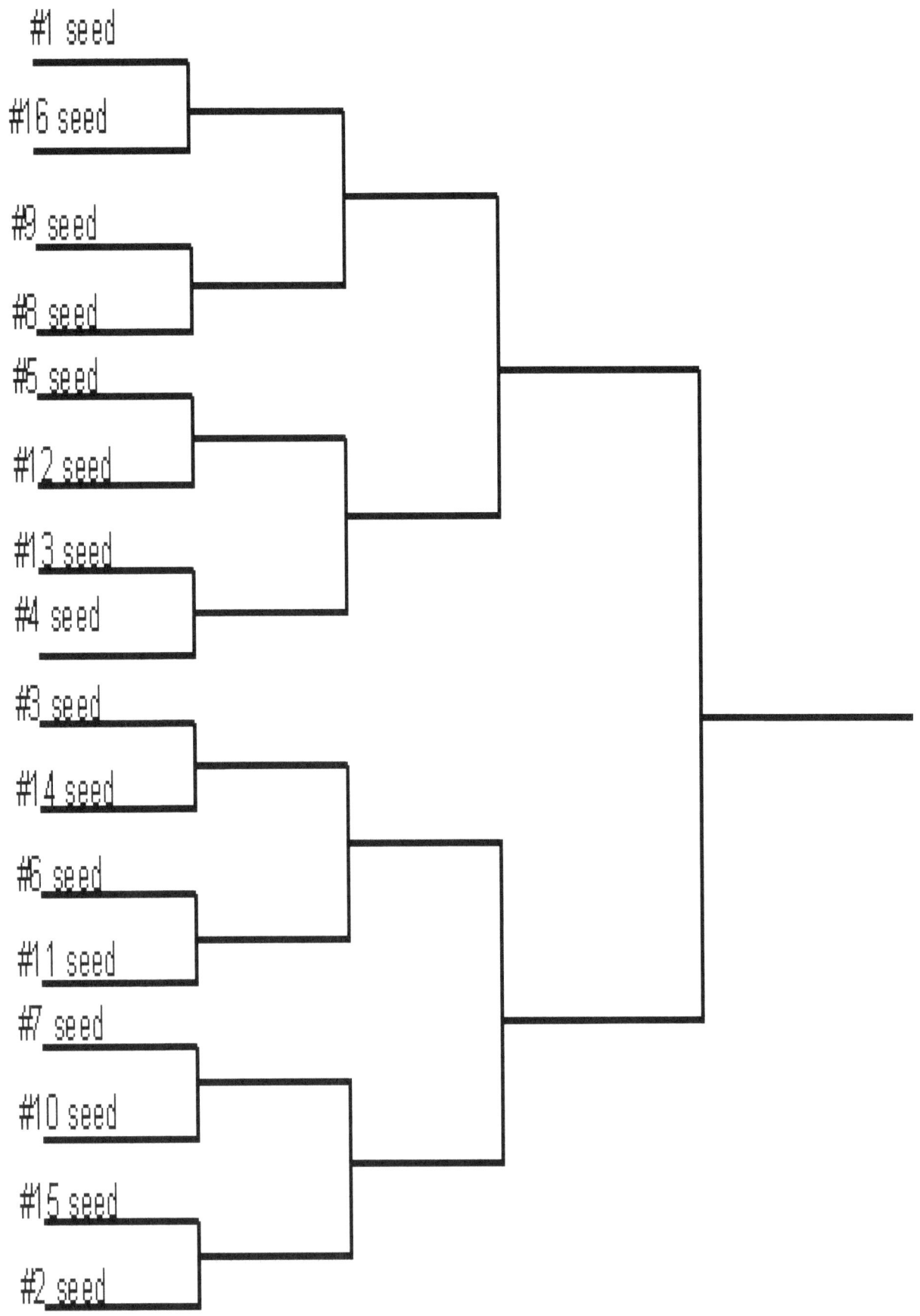

In district's, he was 5th seated. The 4th and 5th seated wrestlers are on the same side of the chart, in which is a wrestler he could barely beat. He was to wrestle him the second match. Even then if he beats him The next match was against the 1st seated wrestler who was ranked in the state, in which he had no chance of beating.

He also had no chance of beating the 2nd seated wrestler, who also is rank in the state. This wrestler is on the other side of the chart. Which he wouldn't wrestle against, unless he advanced to the final round of the tournament.

The tournament advanced to his weight class. At the beginning of the first round. You can see the 1st seated wrestler is the first match of the weight class. That's when a strange thing happened. The 1st seated wrestler, who is ranked in the state was pinned in less than 30 seconds to an unseeded wrestler. Us as coaches was like if our wrestler wins his two matches. He'll make it to regional's. He did win his first round match. The weight class advanced to the last match of the weight class. This is the 2nd seated wrestler.

A strange thing happened again. The 2nd seated wrestler got pinned in less than 30 seconds. It just so happened, all of us coaches for our wrestler was standing next to each other when that happened. We looked at each other, and said he's going to state. Referring to our wrestler. As fate would have it. My wrestler ended up placing 2nd in district's, 3rd in regional's and ended as a All State wrestler. This was all due to the events that happened in district's.

THE next wrestler is a kid, I coached his whole wrestling career. Now this kid was very book smart I was going to college on his academics I definitely wasn't going on his athletic ability the four years I costume she didn't win a match too almost to end of his junior year all the matches he lost or JV matches which none of them were closed he always got pinned or gave up a lot of points.

The one thing I must say he never gave up it always kept pushing his self I used to even say to myself why is he even out here he doesn't have an ounce of talent or athletic ability going into his senior year he became the varsity wrestler because no one else was at the weight I knew the team couldn't count on him for a win because of the previous years.

As his senior season started, he won his first match of that year and the next match, then match after match. Mind you, his skills hadn't got much better, he just was a hard worker. He just kept winning. I couldn't believe what I was seeing. You know anything about wrestling. You can only do a move one time whether you score or not.

For some strange reason, he was able to do this particular move over and over. It's not a super great move. It.s your basic move, but he would score with most of the time. I could never understand that. He always lost to this one wrestler from the High School I wrestle for and coached. This wrestler would destroy him all the time. Most of his losses is to him.

He was a low seed in districts, but somehow he placed in the top 4 in order to go to Regionals. In regionals, he was also able to make it out. I just didn't see how this is happening. In districts and regionals, he ran across that same kid again who always mopped him up.

At the state tournament. I just figured well he made it to the state tournament that's good for him. It didn't end there. He lost his first match bad. He was able to wrestle back to the placing rounds of the tournament and become a All State wrestler. On his way to the placing rounds of the state tournament. He had to wrestle the kid who always beat him from my high school. They both had to win the match in order be considered an All-State wrestler. I knew he couldn't beat this kid. Wouldn't you know it he handled the kid, using the same move over.

He beat him by a wide margin. I couldn't believe this kid placed. I even asked the wrestler from my high school that he beat, what happened? He said. I just don't know, I couldn't stop the move, I don't just don't know what happened.

He invited me to his graduation party. At the party. He came up to me and asked me. Coach you think I can wrestle in college? First thing came out my mouth. NOPE!!! I said get your education and be something. He said right and we both laughed.

He is now making way more money than his high school teammates.

The final wrestler is a kid I coached for 2 of his 4 years in high school. But always kept up with his wrestling. He was a decent wrestler. The 2 years I coached him which was his freshman and sophomore years. He did well a little above average. He didn't qualify for the state tournament neither one of those years. In his junior year.

This time I was coaching another school but kept track of how he was doing. He pretty much was having the same season as he did the 2 previous seasons. But this time he qualified for regional's. I was able to come see him wrestle in regional's.

In regional's a wrestler has to win 2 matches before he loose 2 matches. He lost his first match. Now he has to win the next 2 matches in order to qualify for the state tournament, What happened the next 2 matches, I believe will never happen again. The wrestler he was to wrestle next had forfeited the match. So now he just has to win one more match to be a state qualifier.

While watching this one match, in which he would wrestle the loser of that match. He could not beat either wrestler. I could see on his face. He knew he wasn't going to qualify for the state tournament. Has that match was nearing to the end. Something happened I never seen before or since.

The wrestler who was winning the match, did what is called an illegal slam. The that gets slammed and can not continue on in the match. The slammed wrestler wins. Not only he couldn't wrestle, he was carried out by ambulance and could not finish the tournament. The wrestler that did the slam was disqualified from the regional tournament. As fate would have it.

The wrestler I had coached, had no one to wrestle. So he automatically qualified to the state tournament and to the final round of the regional tournament. He lost that match. He is the first wrestler I've ever seen, qualify for the state tournament without winning a match in regional. Talk about fate.

What each one these wrestlers have in common. Is they all where hard workers and gave up on themselves. Just by them never giving up on themselves and believing things will work out. Sure enough it did.

In life. You'll be faced with people and obstacles, that you see no-way around. As, long as you're doing everything you can to better your life. Just know, by you not totally giving up or listening to the wrong people. Things just tend to work their way out supernaturally.

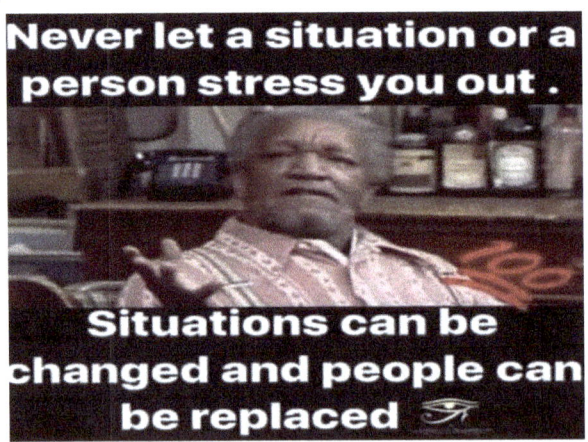

This chapter is inspired by somebody, I'm very close and dear to. With plans to marry. Her name is beside the title, Ashley Bowman.

I've debated about this chapter for a couple of years. I was worried it would hurt my wrestlers feelings. So I didn't put this chapter in the book, plus I didn't know what to name this chapter.

Watching her, as a single mom of 3 kids under the age of 10. With really no outside help and having health issues, living paycheck-to-paycheck. She literally has issues she faces every single day. Either with the kids, family, job or health. But still manages to persevere and make things happen for herself.

I see this with my own eyes all the time. Some issues I saw. There is no way of it working out and somehow miraculously they work out to my surprise. I see her as an example for all the other women and men out there doing what it takes to make it happen, by never giving up, when facing major obstacles and somehow another things just works out for them.

I see these type of people as having great **FAITH** and belief that things will work out for them. If you only take one thing from this book. Remember, never to give up, persevere and things will happen.

I asked her what's her secret? She said perseverance. That's how I came up with the title for this chapter.

Keep it Pushing no-matter what...

Life Questions

1. What would I want to experience if money was not a issue?
2. How do I want to grow?
3. What will I contribute to this world?
4. Who am I Why am I here?
5. Where am I going? How will I be remembered?
6. If I achieve all my life goals. How will I feel? How can I feel that along the way?
7. What has the most importance in my life? What and who do I value most? What am I passionate about?
8. What brings the most joy and peace in my life?
9. What does a successful life look like for me?
10. What do others most admire in me? What unique gifts do I want to share with everyone. I you don't know ask 5 people who know you well.
11. What are my top 10 achievements in life?

Set 40 Goals in all areas of your life.

1. _____
2. _____
3. _____
4. _____
5. _____
6. _____
7. _____
8. _____
9. _____
10. _____
11. _____
12. _____
13. _____
14. _____
15. _____
16. _____
17. _____
18. _____
19. _____
20. _____

21. _____
22. _____
23. _____
24. _____
25. _____
26. _____
27. _____
28. _____
29. _____
30. _____
31. _____
32. _____
33. _____
34. _____
35. _____
36. _____
37. _____
38. _____
39. _____
40. _____

Add more on next page.

Goals

Note:
The Book of Proverbs has 31 chapters. I read a chapter a day, for each day of the month. Example; For the first day of the month, I read chapter 1, for the second day of the month I read chapter 2 etc. The chapters are not long at all. You don't have to be religious or believe in God to read the Book of Proverbs. You'll find everything you want to know and gain much knowledge to help you in everyday life in this book.

VISION BOARD

The MAT Merchandise...

Sharing O.J.

Flow like a river
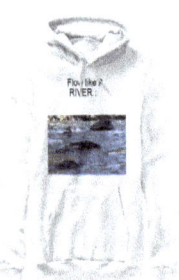

Chicken Sh**

Putting in work

Socks
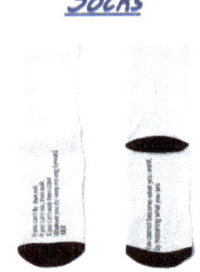

Tights

Mugs

The hand

Checkout the match of Life store.

At

timothydmitchell.com

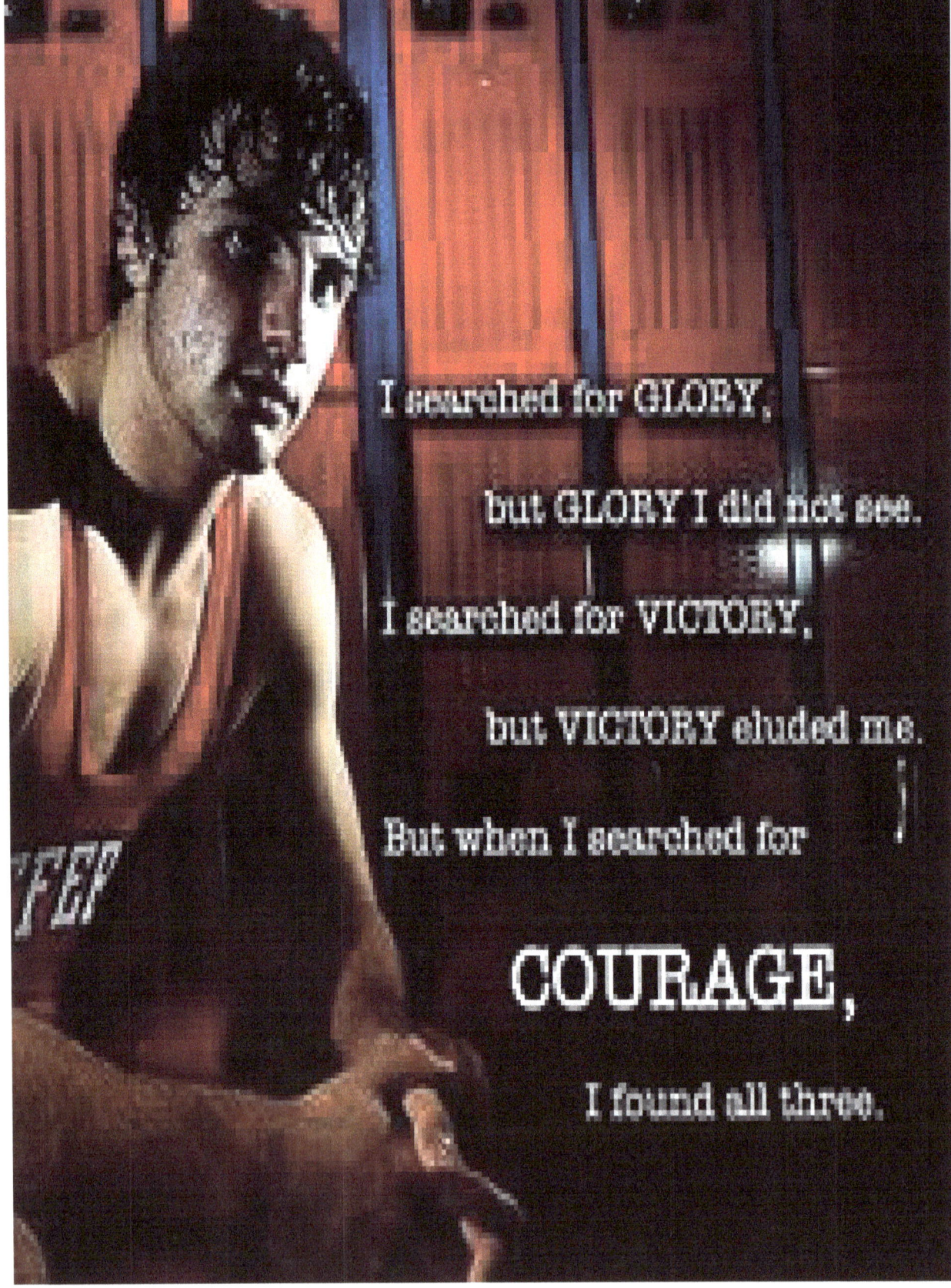

Say it to the hand

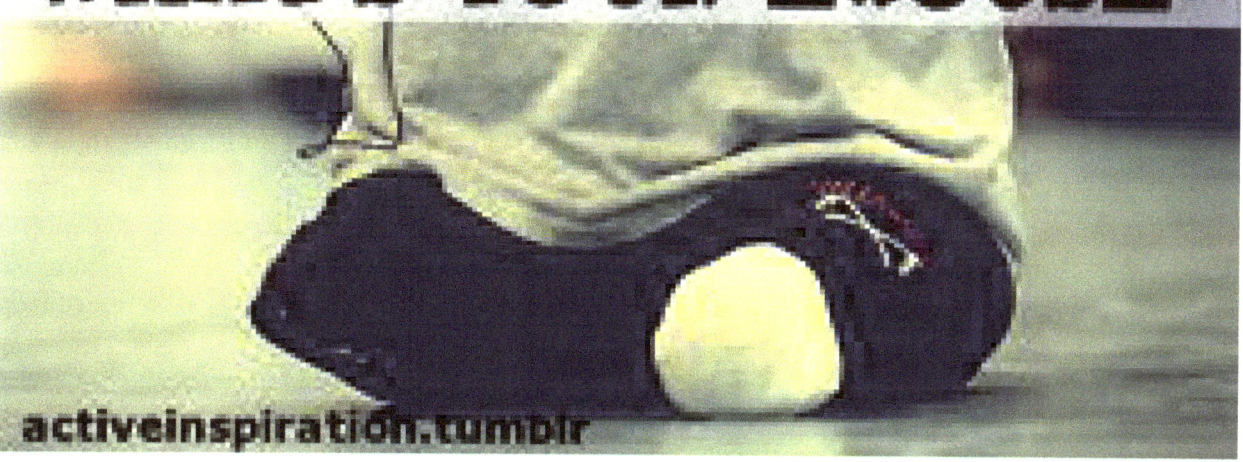

IF YOU'RE TIRED OF STARTING OVER STOP GIVING UP

-Unknown

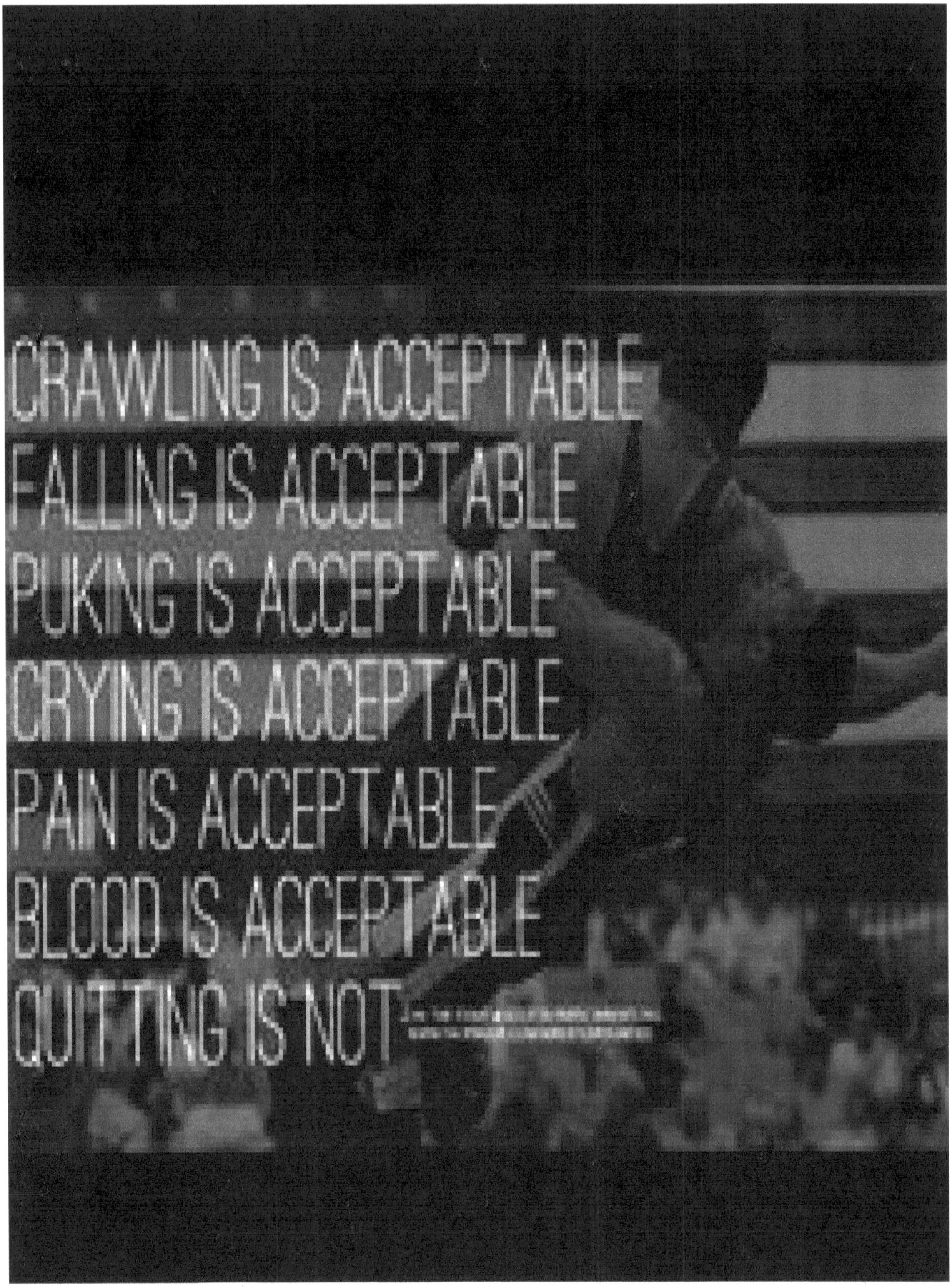

CRAWLING IS ACCEPTABLE
FALLING IS ACCEPTABLE
PUKING IS ACCEPTABLE
CRYING IS ACCEPTABLE
PAIN IS ACCEPTABLE
BLOOD IS ACCEPTABLE
QUITTING IS NOT

"Battle in the Circle"
Willie Madison

A circle is my battlefield
Where I fight to survive without a sword or shield
A war zone where no one gets killed
But where dreams are destroyed and some are revealed
Technique and hard work are my weapons of choice
It's just me and the sound of my coach's voice
I'm a soldier with the desire to win
So give me an opponent and let the battle begin

1983

2018

Lone Wolf

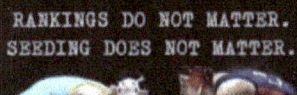

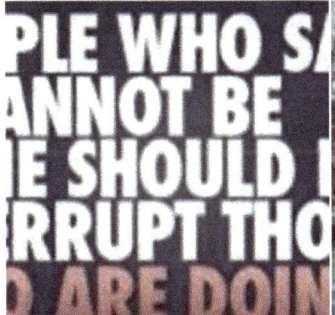
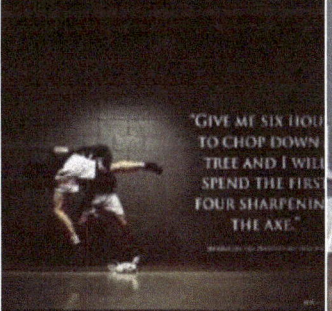

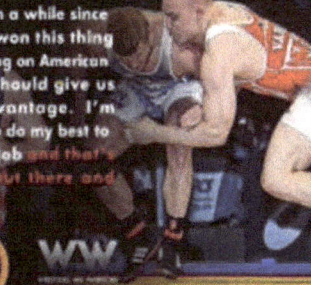

I Sleep On My Stomach Because I Don't Like Being On My Back

Sporting medals earned at state and national tournaments, Wayne Memorial junior Melissa Fogarty (above and at the right is working pose) becomes the first young lady to become the city's, and probably the area's first All-America high school female wrestler. (News article in the Wayne Eagle.)

All-American
This young lady is really tough

By TOM MOORADIAN
Staff Writer

Melissa Fogarty is the kind of teen you'd like living next door.

She's gregarious. Considerate. And is dedicated to the task before her. Oh, you bet, she also blushes when you mention her successes.

This 16-year-old Wayne Memorial Junior has set some high goals and standards in her personal life. And one of those she reached over the weekend in Ann Arbor.

She is All America in one of the most growing sports there is — wrestling.

That's right — that's not a typographical error.

"I would like to be the best in what I do, and help others while doing it," says Fogarty, a 132-pound bundle of strength and determination.

Fogarty also happens to be a pathfinder. She is the first Wayne athlete, and probably first in the area to be awarded the All-America designation as a high school female wrestler.

And Melissa did it the

See **MELISSA**, page A

Sometimes it takes a person years to become a overnight success.-Prince

I AM GONNA SHOW YOU HOW GREAT I AM

Muhammad Ali

This is what happens when you go after your

DREAMS

Give it all you got. All the time.

WHEN YOU WANT TO SUCCEED AS BAD AS YOU WANT TO BREATHE, THEN YOU'LL BE SUCCESSFUL.

LEAVE IT ALL ON THE MAT!

www.ingramcontent.com/pod-product-compliance
Lightning Source LLC
Chambersburg PA
CBHW061748290426
44108CB00028B/2925